DATE DUE

Aug 14, 2018	

GAYLORD — PRINTED IN U.S.A.

Murder in Married Life

This is a novel of classical detection in a cheerful vein, though its people are real and its events plausible.

It is narrated by Tessa Price (Tessa Crichton of *Death in the Grand Manor* has now married Robin Price of the Metropolitan C.I.D.) and the root of the plot is blackmail. Information from her husband, and from some curious acquaintances out of her own past who are evidently connected with the case, leads Tessa herself to become (rather willingly) involved; and being almost as shrewd as she is mischievous she begins to draw various conclusions, not all of them correct.

Many of the encounters in the story take place during Tessa's visits to a London department store, on the top floor of which is a bar to which any customer who spends over twenty-five pounds is invited for a drink. Here lies part of the secret which, in its overt and practised form, is bedevilling Robin at Scotland Yard – who hates blackmailers more than any other criminals.

Tessa gets a bit too knowing, and it is her own life that is finally at stake.

Reviews of Anne Morice's first crime novel, *Death in the Grand Manor*, are printed on the back of this book's wrapper. This, her second, provides the same ingredients of gaiety, good characterisation, ingenuity, mystery and terror.

By the same author

DEATH IN THE GRAND MANOR

Murder in Married Life

ANNE MORICE

Macmillan

© Anne Morice 1971

All rights reserved. No part of this publication may be reproduced or transmitted, in any form or by any means, without permission.

SBN Boards: 333 12576 2

First published 1971 by
MACMILLAN LONDON LTD
London and Basingstoke
Associated companies in New York Toronto
Dublin Melbourne Johannesburg & Madras

Printed in Great Britain by
RICHARD CLAY (THE CHAUCER PRESS) LTD
Bungay, Suffolk

One

Having forsaken all others, in a manner of speaking, in order to cleave only unto one Robin Price of the Dedley C.I.D., I had resigned myself to a life of obscurity and domestic bliss in our picturesque and damp little cottage at Storhampton-on-Thames. However, one year of marriage had taught us both that there is more than one way of achieving domestic bliss, and the claims of a double income and two separate careers are not to be lightly tossed aside.

Among those whom I had not totally forsaken was an Anglo-American film company, in one of whose productions I had once figured in a modest way, and I believe that Robin and I were about equally relieved when they offered me a three-year contract at a far from modest salary. It is true that having tied me up to their own satisfaction they promptly lost all interest in the transaction, but the salary, less ten per cent agent's commission, was paid regularly into my bank account at the precise period of our lives when hard cash was the most pressing need.

It had happened that at almost the identical time when I was signing on the dotted line Robin had received his own step up in the world, in the form of promotion to the Metropolitan Branch; and our new affluence enabled us to begin life in Beacon Square, S.W.1, in the style to which we were both so eager to become accustomed.

It was not the most fruitful and creative stage in my

career, but at least the enforced idleness gave me plenty of time for self-indulgent shopping expeditions in search of furnishings for our pretty new house, so I did not complain more than a dozen times a day. Moreover, without it, I might never have taken a hand in the real life drama of Mr B, the vanishing book carrier, and the capricious behaviour of the telephone. Who can say how far the course of justice might then have gone astray, or, more to the point, who would now be here to tell the tale?

(ii)

One store which became a favourite hunting ground was called Thurgoods. It lay between Soho and Piccadilly Circus and combined a variety of moods and merchandise under one roof.

The ground floor, mysteriously known as the Boutique, was a glorious hotch-potch of Thai silk, trendy modern furniture, Indian jewellery and Italian straw bags; and to this extent, I suppose, offered no more than a dozen other shops in that part of London. However, these were only a sample of the wonders to be found within. On the first floor was a separate department dealing exclusively in second-hand furniture and bric-a-brac. Three-quarters of the customers who swarmed into the ground floor never entered the treasure trove above. Whereas a lift just inside the main door enabled the collector and connoisseur to whisk himself straight to the upper haunts, without so much as a glimpse of all the gimmickries down below.

I was among the few who patronised both departments, though my first-floor visits were primarily of a social character, since an old family friend, Betty

Haverstock, had recently been put in charge of it. It was from her that I first learnt of the existence of even more rarefied premises on the floor above that.

Betty's expert knowledge of antiques had been acquired in the natural course of things, through a series of marriages into families whose town and country houses were bulging with the stuff. Beginning this rewarding career in a run-down Irish manor house, she had landed up, ten years and three husbands later, on a sizeable chunk of Caribbean coastline. On this site Betty had constructed a pleasure dome of great magnificence, and the story went that, one morning, an American millionaire had turned up on the doorstep and asked to be shown around. He became so enraptured with the place that he could hardly tear himself away, and was invited to stay for lunch. Two hours later, over coffee and cognac in the Italian pavilion, the property changed hands, and a week later the new owner took possession. History did not relate whether the husband had been thrown in along with the rest of the contents, but Betty had returned to London alone, and with no visible signs of affluence to show for her pains.

She had taken her job with Thurgoods in order to put her vast experience to profitable account, and also, presumably, while waiting for husband number five.

In spite of my regular visits, I rarely succeeded in buying anything on the first floor, for Betty had a forceful character whose full forcefulness was normally fixed on preventing my doing so. However, one morning she did an about-turn and brought out all her big guns on behalf of a spindly little book carrier, for which I had no use whatever.

'Don't be an idiot, Tessa,' she said impatiently. 'It's genuine eighteenth century and in perfect condition.

Only thirty-five guineas, and I guarantee it would fetch twice that at auction.'

'But I hardly ever carry books around,' I protested. 'And, if I did, I should think a plastic bag would be much more practical.'

'Don't be so ignorant. It's a sort of portable shelf. You could put the telephone directories in it, if you wanted to be terribly vulgar. You'd be entitled to a free drink, if you bought it,' she added, looking at her watch.

'I should think I'd be entitled to free psycho-analysis. Do you keep a bottle in the staff cloakroom?'

'No, but there's plenty upstairs. Haven't you ever seen the Boardroom?'

'Never, now you mention it.'

'That shows what a rotten customer you are. Anyone who spends over twenty-five quid at one go is entitled to a free drink up there.'

'What a fantastic idea! What's the point of pouring all the profits down the customers' throats?'

'Don't be fooled. Half the customers are like you; terribly timid and suspicious. They think there must be a catch, and nothing will get them near the place. The other half buys a mass of things they can't afford, just because there's a few bobs' worth of free gin thrown in.'

'I take it there's also a contingent who make a habit of dropping in whenever they feel a thirst coming on?'

'A few do,' she admitted. 'One, in particular; but they're personal friends of the management. The barman has a most elaborate set of rules for keeping out the real gatecrashers.'

'Don't tell me they actually keep a barman?'

'Well, not a real one, no, because it's not a real job. He used to be a sort of family retainer, and they've more or less put him out to grass on the second floor. Of course, they do some of their private entertaining there, too, specially our Mr Arthur, but it's really a sinecure. It's one of the few endearing things one hears on the staff grapevine; the way they look after old Barnes, I mean. I think our Daddy Chairman must be at the bottom of it. He's quite an old duck, when you get to know him.'

'Not a widower, by any chance?' I asked, scenting romance.

'Don't be crude, Tessa.'

'Okay, but who's Mr Arthur?'

'Elder son. Pa is chairman and managing director. The younger son is called Mr Teddy, and he's in charge of all that trash on the ground floor. Mrs Teddy does most of the work, but he's nominally in charge. Anything else you'd like to know?'

'No, thanks. It all sounds very cosy.'

Betty looked at me speculatively, then said: 'That's just the public image, I'm afraid. Behind the scenes they fight like cats and dogs. There's a gigantic row boiling up at the moment, by all accounts, and I wouldn't half mind finding out what it's all about. In fact, that's rather what I had you in mind for.'

'Indeed? What was my role?'

'I thought, if I took you up and introduced you to Mr Arthur, who's always around at this hour, you might strike up a beautiful friendship. He's a sucker for what he calls the dolly birds. You'd have him crying on your shoulder in no time.'

'To what end?' I inquired, not much attracted to this programme. 'Don't tell me you're taking up blackmail, as a sideline?'

This feeble joke got an even frostier reception than it deserved, and to make amends I said heavily: 'Okay,

Betty, wrap the silly thing up and I'll take it. What's another thirty-five quid between friends?'

'Guineas.'

'Guineas, then; but, on second thoughts, can you send it? I'm on my way to a swanky lunch and it might look rather affected to march in with a book carrier in my hand.'

'The van's gone for today, but I could get it on tomorrow's delivery.'

'No hurry,' I assured her.

'Will there be someone to take it in?'

'Bound to be.'

'I mean someone reliable; not that silly creature who answers the telephone.'

'No, Sandy will be there tomorrow. You could hardly get more reliable than that, could you?'

'No, you couldn't,' Betty agreed, with conviction, and began making out the bill.

I handed her my cheque, which she scrutinised carefully, then waved me towards the lift. She followed me inside and pressed the top button. Curiously enough, I found myself growing steadily more timid and suspicious as we sailed up to the second floor.

(iii)

'It was the full anti-climax, though, because we landed up in the most normal, uncreepy room imaginable,' I admitted, when describing the incident at dinner, which was elegantly served to us by the so-called silly creature. This was a young man named Sebastian, who was rather more gainfully employed in this capacity than he deserved to be, a nasty tumble having temporarily interrupted his career in the *corps de ballet*. He could not truthfully have been described as one of

Nature's gentlemen's gentlemen, being both slapdash and temperamental, as well as a picker-up of unconsidered trifles. To be fair, though, he had either curbed this habit, or become more skilful at it, after learning that the master of the house was a professional thief-catcher.

'It was just what you would imagine a boardroom to be,' I went on. 'Large table, centre, and a few rather dingy chairs dotted around. In fact, the only oddity was this very modern bar in one corner of the room, bang opposite the lift. It was all glass and chromium and it looked wildly out of place; but, of course, it would. It was only installed a few years ago.'

'Any bold and trusting customers present?' Robin asked.

'Not one. The barman was there all right, but he looked rather like a Victorian elder statesman, and he could hardly drag his eyes away from the racing page. There was another man, about the same age, in one corner of the room. I can't tell you much about him because he was mostly hidden by a copy of the *Psychical Times*.'

'You mean "Financial", surely?'

'No, that begins with an F, doesn't it?'

'Well, never mind. Since he was hidden behind it, how could you tell his age?'

'I could see his hands, and they were pudgy and elderly. His legs were the same, with the sort of shoes and socks which no one under the age of sixty would be seen dead in.'

Robin laughed: 'Honestly, Tessa, I sometimes wish I had you on my staff. We could use your powers of perception.'

'Laugh away,' I said, 'but there was just one detail which might have escaped the layman.'

'Which layman are we speaking of now?'

'Any old layman who wasn't a pro. He might not have noticed that old podge wasn't reading his paper at all; only pretending to.'

'That's nothing. I'd have done just the same, myself. How do you know he wasn't?'

'It was the self-conscious way he held it. He reminded me of an actor, waiting for his cue.'

'And did it come?'

'Apparently not. He was still stuck there when I left.'

'Well, it all sounds pretty tame, I agree.'

'Ah, but I've kept the best bit for the end. There was another man there, sitting all solitary and hunched up by the bar, and you'll never guess who he was.'

'I'm sure I won't.'

'Julian Brown. Remember?'

'No, and I thought you said there weren't any customers.'

'Oh, Julian wasn't a customer; he's one of the bosses. The business belongs to his family. I suppose they bought it up and didn't bother to change the name.'

'And Julian is yet another son?'

'Yes and no.'

'It must be one or the other, surely?'

'He's two sons, as it happens. Oh, you must remember him? He's been around for years.'

'Not in my circles.'

'Well, he was in mine, for a brief period. He used to go to all the coming-out parties. I expect the Mums invited him because he was so rich and so safe, and, of course, unattached. God knows what he got out of it, though. He was years older than the rest of us, even then; he must be at least forty now. And the silly part was that, in spite of being such a dedicated party-goer, socially he was a dead loss. Not an atom of humour and it was like dancing with an amorous ironing board.'

'Poor fellow!'

'Pathetic. He was a crashing snob, too.'

'Married?'

'Never, as far as I know, but I lost touch with him years ago. He never fancied me, I'm thankful to say. Now, he suddenly bobs up again, disguised as Mr Arthur.'

'Oh, so they're the same chap?'

'A walking, talking schizo. What happened was that, when we arrived upstairs, Betty handed the barman two copies of my bill. He stuck one of them on that spiky thing, then initialled the other and gave it back to her. Meanwhile, Julian and I had gone through our scene of recognising each other, and "Fancy that!" and everything, and Betty said: "I see you two already know each other, so I'll beat it back to the treadmill," and off she hopped. Then the barman asked me what I wanted and I said gin and tonic, and that was it. Most unnerving.'

'I can't see why.'

'Well, for one thing, Julian hadn't changed at all. Just as gauche and tongue-tied, and it had the same effect on me. I dried up completely. Old Fatty behind the newspaper obviously had both ears cocked, which didn't make things any easier; and, of course, I'd chosen quite the wrong drink. It's physically impossible to get all that tonic down in a couple of gulps. As it was, about half of it shot up my nose because, when we'd been sitting there in this grisly silence for about five minutes, Julian suddenly glared at me and invited me to lunch.'

'Perhaps he had matters to discuss which he did not want the newspaper man to overhear?'

'Very likely, but it was exactly the way he did things

in the old days. No finesse, I suppose, although I'm sure he intended to appear frightfully bold and dashing.'

'And did you accept the invitation?'

'No, I explained that I already had a lunch date, so he calmly asked me to make it tomorrow, instead?'

'And you said Yes?'

'No, I didn't. Tomorrow is Wednesday and Sandy will be here. He probably thought I was inventing excuses, but he's conditioned to rebuffs of that kind; they feed his persecution mania. We finally fixed it for Thursday. For one thing, I thought Betty would be pleased.'

'Where is he taking you?'

'Oh, the Savoy, you may be sure. It was always the Savoy. I should think they've put up a plaque to him by now.'

'And have you told Betty?'

'Not yet. I looked in, on my way out, but she'd got a customer. I said I'd call her in the morning, and I will, too. I should think she'd be jumping for joy at the way things have turned out, wouldn't you?'

'Frankly, I don't care whether she is or not. I'd rather she did her own dirty work, instead of using you for some devious purpose of her own.'

'Oh, that's unfair, Robin. If you'd ever met Betty, you'd know that she's the most straightforward person who ever lived. She can be tough, I admit, but never devious. The trouble is, you're beginning to see criminal tendencies in everyone these days.'

Not for the first time, he neatly chopped the ground from under my feet by admitting the truth of this.

'It's an occupational hazard,' he said. 'We are all prone to them. You, for instance, are quite capable of making a three-act drama out of the potatoes boiling dry.'

How salutary, as someone once remarked, to see ourselves as others see us – however distorted the picture.

Two

High among the blessings bestowed by our new prosperity were the weekly visits of Miss Phelps Sanderson, inevitably, though inappropriately, known to one and all as Sandy.

She had been recommended to me by Betty, in one of whose households she had operated for a brief spell and, in theory, she came to 'help' me with my fanmail. However, it must be admitted that this, as yet, would not have provided a full day's work, even for someone far less efficient than Sandy, and, in fact, she had soon taken over other departments as well. In addition to my tangled income tax web, she dealt with the housekeeping accounts, organised our parties, coped with appointments and press interviews, and generally became so indispensable that after only a month of her regime I was going around asking everyone how I had ever managed without her.

That I might, at any moment, be called upon to do so was the constant reminder of Betty who pointed out, with depressing regularity, that it was no accident that such a pearl beyond price had not been snapped up by the highest in the land. In short, there was a formidable fly in the ointment, in the form of an invalid mother.

Sandy, herself, was a large-boned, powerfully built woman, who had risen to dizzy heights in the Women's Army Corps during the war; though, like many people of massive proportions, she surrounded herself with miniature objects. She worked on a toylike, portable typewriter, went in for tiny clips and brooches and crawled in and out of her Mini Morris like a turtle who had been carelessly fitted out with a tortoise shell.

Very likely her mother was built on the same lines and had also been an athletic type in her youth, for she was known as Bobs. Unfortunately, by the time they came into my life, the only exercise left to Bobs was finding out what Sandy liked and promptly putting a stop to it.

So successfully had this campaign been waged that poor Sandy was now reduced to working on one day a week for three separate employers, although always on the strict understanding that the arrangement could be terminated at a moment's notice.

Perhaps Bobs believed there was safety in numbers, and preferred Sandy's professional loyalties to be divided between three camps, but, nevertheless, some remnants of insecurity must have lingered. I soon learnt that my two current fellow-employers dated from only a month or two back, and that one was already growing fidgety, owing to the frequency with which Sandy had been forced to let her down.

Taking stock of the situation, I prepared some counter-measures. I dismissed the idea of informing Sandy that her mother was a selfish old brute, who should be treated accordingly, concluding that this routine had been worked to death by all my predecessors and that my voice was unlikely to be any more persuasive. Instead, I attacked the problem at its source and questioned Sandy exhaustively on every imaginable aspect of Bobs's tastes and temperament. She was reluctant at first to part with the information, evidently distrusting my motives, as well she might. However, I invented some farrago about being keen as mustard to get an insight into the mentality of different age groups, so as to enlarge the scope of my dramatic portrayals, etcetera, and she must have swallowed it, for she flung herself into the spirit of the thing, with typical verve and enthusiasm.

As I had surmised, there was nothing of the Dresden china about this particular little old lady. She was more of a retired Boadicea waging an implacable armchair-war against, predictably enough, immigrants, civil servants, motorists, pedestrians, abstract art, pop music and central heating.

I mentally filed this anthology for future reference, while concentrating on such aspects of daily life as met with her approval. They included: her Yorkshire terrier, the works of Gilbert and Sullivan, smoked salmon and a nice glass of wine with her dinner.

'She doesn't suffer from any internal complaint, then?' I asked, on hearing of the last two items.

'No, thank the Lord. Arthritis is bad enough; beastly painful, too.'

'Is she completely chair-bound?'

'Oh, we have our good days, too. We even managed Wimbledon one day last summer. It was a shame that both the matches we saw were between the Aussies, but otherwise we enjoyed every moment of it.'

Sandy identified herself so closely with her mother that it was not always possible to tell whether the 'we', which figured so prominently in her conversation, referred to both of them, or specifically to Bobs. The distinction, however, was hardly worth making, for my tactics were based on the premise that by pleasing Bobs I should please them both. The next day I laid out my first capital investment; cash down, too, to avoid any embarrassing records.

The following Wednesday, when we had completed our business chores, and before Sandy could launch herself on to the mini typewriter, I said: 'And now you must help me to plan a dinner party. For about twenty, I should think.'

'Yours to command, old top. Just cough up the list of invites.'

'Oh, just so long as they're gluttons for the smoked salmon,' I said. 'Some misguided friend has sent us about a ton of the stuff. You could start with my agent. She always has a splendid appetite.'

I was rewarded for my guile by the sight of a wistful expression on Sandy's moonlike face, so I whipped up the agony, by throwing out a few more names at random, then suddenly rocked backwards, saying: 'Oh gracious, what a fool! I remember now that your mother is rather keen on smoked salmon, isn't she? I suppose you wouldn't be an absolute angel ...'

It was quite a performance, and it worked. No further reference was made to the party, and the first bolt had been shot.

Although I was careful not to copy the formula too slavishly, it was weird how often kind friends came up with cases of wine, recordings of the Gondoliers, etcetera, and tickets for plays which had evidently been written with the sole object of bringing joy into the lives of disagreeable and arthritic old women.

That I had not overestimated the need for these costly and elaborate measures was borne out by the fact that during the first six weeks of Sandy's reign two of her other weekly jobs came to an end. She quickly found others, but, on the day after my unexpected reunion with Julian Brown, there were signs that the axe was about to fall in yet another quarter.

Sandy had let herself into the house punctually at nine, just as Sebastian pranced in and plopped a breakfast tray on my bed, and for the next hour I heard her lumbering about in the little sitting-room next door, her movements punctuated by clackety bursts on the typewriter.

At ten o'clock, according to custom, she tapped on the door and entered, carrying a pile of letters.

'No peace for the wicked,' she announced cheerfully. 'And a very good morning to you!'

'Pull up a pew,' I said, glancing through the post. I often used this sporty vernacular with Sandy, for I guessed it had a familiar ring for her, and it afforded me a certain amount of private amusement as well.

The letters had already been opened and sorted, and many had suggestions and comments appended to them.

'How's Bobs?' I inquired of this jewel among amanuenses. It was the routine question and one she never seemed to tire of answering. On this occasion the response was not encouraging.

'Dicey, I'm afraid. We've had one of our bad turns.'

'Turns?' I repeated. 'I didn't know arthritis came in turns.'

She smiled unhappily: 'True 'nuff, but there are side effects, you know. Fact is, the old ticker's beginning to wear out.'

'You mean, her heart ... ?'

'Definitely wonky. Still, mustn't grumble. We'd be worse off at sea, I daresay.'

I could hardly see that she would have been, but let it pass.

'Is it serious?'

'Well, we seem to be out of the wood now. We weren't feeling too clever over the weekend, and Sunday night was rotten. We definitely couldn't have been left alone on Monday. The doctor said it would be all right, but I wasn't having any, thank you very much.'

'What about your neighbour? I thought she was good about popping in, and so on?'

'Ha!' Sandy said bitterly. 'A sight too good, if you ask me. Bobs heard someone creeping about the other day, and, when she went to investigate, there was our Mrs Goldsmith, as bold as brass in the kitchen, with the fridge door wide open. She'd let herself in with the key I gave her for emergencies, and she had some tale about having seen the milk outside, but Bobs said she coloured right up when she spoke to her and slammed out in a huff, which just shows you. Anyway, I wasn't risking a repeat of that, so I rang Mrs Haynes and said I couldn't manage my day with her.'

'That's your Monday job? The home-made cake and chocolate woman?'

'That's right. I do her books, and a right old shambles they were in, I can tell you.'

'Was she cross?'

Sandy pursed her lips. 'That's putting it mildly. You'd have thought it was the end of the world. She even had the nerve to hint that Bobs ought to be in a nursing home. I ask you! Poor old Bobs to be carted off to some rotten institution, just so that Mrs Haynes's precious accounts shouldn't suffer. That'll be the day!'

'I expect she was a bit rattled because she depends on you, and, to that extent I can sympathise,' I said, picking my words carefully. 'But no one would be so foolish, or so unkind, as to grudge you a day off, in a crisis. I know I wouldn't.'

She planted herself squarely at the foot of my bed: 'Fact is, they're not all such decent sticks as you, more's the pity,' she said, flushing hotly in her embarrassment at handing out this flowery compliment. 'Oh well, this isn't getting the parsnips buttered, is it. I must tank off, back to the grindstone.'

'Oh, by the way, Sandy,' I called after her. 'If a parcel

arrives from Thurgoods will you unpack it specially carefully? It is a book carrier, the like of which we may never see again.'

'Will cope,' she assented, tanking off.

(ii)

The day had turned full cycle and I was in bed, once more, by the time Robin returned. He had telephoned to say he was working late and would not be home for dinner.

I had striven to keep awake because I could not wait to tell him that Bobs had a wonky ticker; but I was obliged to repeat the phrase three times before he could take it in. Clearly, there were more important matters on his mind.

'Difficult case?' I asked.

'A real brute.'

'Someone been knocked off?'

'Not so far, though someone is certainly asking for it.'

I studied this enigma in silence, asking myself why he had to work late and arrive home in a black mood on account of a crime which had yet to be committed. Had I not been so sleepy, I should have found the answer without prompting. Blackmailers, besides being Robin's most hated criminals, were, I was told, a difficult variety to catch.

'Will you get him?'

'Not without a lot more luck than we've had so far.'

'I suppose the victim has no idea who's doing the blackmailing?'

'So she claims. Also that she was fatheaded enough to pay up on the first demand. It was only when he started putting the screws on again that she came along to pour it all out to Auntie Scotland Yard.'

'But there must have been some contact? How did he approach her, for instance?'

'By telephone; except for the final instructions. No way of tracing the calls, and she didn't recognise the voice. Could have been a man disguised as a woman, or vice versa.'

'Servants?'

'No, this is in the big-time, professional class; none of your little amateur snoopers trying to squeeze a few hundred quid.'

'And what about those final instructions?'

'On a postcard; the kind you buy ready stamped. Message printed with an ordinary cheap ballpoint.'

'All the same, why the change of method?'

'Well, I agree it seems unnecessary on the face of it, but you have to consider the risks of telephoning a message of that kind. The victim would be in an advanced state of nervous tension. She might think she'd got it clear, but wouldn't some doubts soon creep in? The instructions were fairly complicated, and he couldn't afford the tiniest deviation or mistiming on her part. The only completely safe thing was to write it down for her.'

'And no leads at all?'

'None, so far.'

'And she's in a real jam, is she? She couldn't just say: "Publish and be damned"?'

'She won't even contemplate it. It's not simply her own reputation that's at stake. There's a husband involved, too.'

'Well, good for her! I'd feel the same, if it were you and me. And what a challenge for you, darling! When you do lay the finger on him, you'll be the hero of the hour.'

'No, I won't. If we catch him, the affair will be

hushed up. If not, I shall be the scapegoat of the hour.'

'Oh, I'm sure you'll win through, in the end. Is Mrs X anyone I know, by the way?'

'As though I'd tell you, if she were! Oh well, let's talk of something more interesting, shall we?' Robin said, yawning and stretching himself full length on the bed.

Unfortunately, I had to disengage myself to answer the telephone; and I should have known there was only one person in the world who could have chosen that precise moment to ring up.

'Oh, hallo, Julian,' I said.

'What did the lunatic want, at this hour of the night?' Robin asked, when I had rung off.

'He wished to change the venue.'

'Not the Savoy, after all?'

'He thinks it would be nice to meet for a drink at his office first. He has something he wants to show me.'

'Good God!'

'Yes, I thought you'd be surprised, and I must say I can't wait to see what it is.'

'What the hell goes on, Tessa? You claim not to have set eyes on this man for years, and yet here he is, in hot pursuit making idiotic excuses to ring you up at midnight. What does he mean by it?'

'I expect he means something by it, but not what you're implying. There won't be any etchings in Julian's office; or, if there are, I shall jolly well have to look at them. So relax, love, and stop pretending to be a pea-green old bluebottle.'

'I'm not pretending anything,' he said gloomily. 'I am a pea-green old bluebottle.'

But I talked him out of it and the evening ended harmoniously, after all.

Three

Early on Thursday morning I telephoned Thurgoods and asked for Betty.

'I'd have called you, myself,' she said, 'but I didn't think you'd be awake yet.'

'Where's my book carrier?'

'I'm sorry, Tess, but there's been a mix-up.'

'I know there has. You promised to deliver it yesterday.'

'Well, I was mistaken. It wasn't for sale.'

'Whatever can you mean?'

'It turns out to be the personal property of Mrs Teddy. It was only sent to us for cleaning and valuing, but it got put in the stock by mistake. I told you the price was fantastic.'

'That's no consolation if I can't have it.'

'Well, you weren't madly taken with it.'

'I may not have been then, but I am now.'

'How typical! Never mind, I'll look out for a real snip for you, to make up. And just think how lucky you didn't march off with it! I'd have had my cards by now.'

'On the other hand,' I reminded her, 'I should have somewhere to put the telephone directories. I suppose even your Mrs Teddy wouldn't have the nerve to come and snatch it away?'

'I wouldn't put it past her. Listen, Tess, I have to go. I'll credit you with the money, or send your cheque back, whichever you prefer.'

'Don't bother,' I said. 'I'll be in later on this morning and I can pick it up, myself. I'm lunching with the boss.'

There was silence, followed by muffled yaps; then Betty came back on the line and said in a low voice: 'If you get the chance to do it diplomatically, see what you can find out about Jasmine Hawkes.'

'The name rings a faint bell. Who is she?'

'Someone who used to work here.'

'I'll try, Betty, of course; but I can't quite see how it's to be done diplomatically.'

'No, and on second thoughts perhaps you'd better forget the whole thing. These might be rather deep waters.'

It occurred to me as I rang off that it was becoming quite a habit with Betty to saddle me with unwanted things and then withdraw them, just as I was getting interested. However, it soon passed out of my mind, whose full attention was required for choosing a suitable outfit for some etching inspection.

(ii)

The Boardroom presented a livelier face on my second visit. Old Barnes was twirling ice around in a jug, as though to the manner born; and Julian, free from all traces of the Mr Arthur personality, was the centre of a merry, Martini-drinking group.

He rose and came towards the lift as I stepped out, bending over my hand with the familiar, exaggerated gesture. Then, including me in some clandestine fiction of his own, murmured: 'Don't worry, angel; I'll get rid of them as fast as I can.'

I had not been in the least worried, but I could hardly applaud his methods. There can be few less effective ways of dispersing a party of hardened tipplers than to refill their glasses and indicate that there was plenty more to come. And this, no two ways about it, was a particularly hardened crew. It consisted of one man and two women, whose ages I put somewhere in the vast stretches between thirty and forty.

I learnt that the dark, disdainful one was called Joannie Something, and the little fair one Sally Something Else, but I could not pick out a Jasmine or a Hawkes between them. They both acknowledged my presence with well-concealed delight.

The man, who was red-faced and grey-bearded, was named Peregrine Turner, which not only rang a bell but set up a positive carillon. Praise being the coinage of theatrical life, I told him how much I enjoyed his novels. This was untrue, because they were mostly about deformed and moronic people, for ever beating each other up; and even Robin's assurance that they were truthful reflections of some departments of the underworld had done little to convert me.

Unfortunately, this compulsion to make myself agreeable to every new acquaintance gains as many enemies as friends; and, this time, the penalty was Joannie's open hostility. Evidently she had proprietory rights in Peregrine, and didn't care who knew it.

Meanwhile, Julian's foxy little eyes were flashing signals which, rightly or wrongly, I interpreted as a request to cut the cackle, and I was tempted to tell him aloud that he could now relax. Joannie's reactions had clearly shown that with only a dash more cackle from me, and cost what it might in free Martinis, she would have her little party on its feet and out of there in no time at all. The estimate proved correct and, when Peregrine pulled out his diary and wrote down my address, the rout was complete.

Foreseeably, I got no thanks from Julian.

'You made quite a hit with old Perry,' he said patronisingly, when he returned from seeing them into the lift. 'I had no idea you were such a little lion-hunter.'

If I hadn't known him of old, I should have poured the last bubbles of my champagne over his silly head, but I could recall how often such sneering remarks had sprung from ineptitude, rather than malice; so I told him that sticks and stones, etcetera, and that I understood there was something he wanted to show me.

This brought another shifty look from the little close-set eyes, and he said: 'Not so impatient! I'm wondering how far I can trust you.'

'Well, wondering will not provide the answer, any more than I shall.'

'That was rather clever of you,' he murmured, the beady eyes narrowing to slits.

'Oh, do you think so?' I asked, growing bored by these histrionics. 'Well, here's another thing. I think you've provided me with quite enough curiosities for one morning, and furthermore, I'm hungry.'

That clinched it, and beckoning me to follow, he made for the farthest of the four doors from the lift. It opened into a tiny office, crammed to suffocation with goods and chattels. There was a bow window, taking up the whole of one side and, within its curve, a huge desk and a swivel chair. The opposite wall was lined with bookshelves and the top one contained a dozen or more bulging office folders.

Calling over his shoulder for two more of the same, Julian followed me inside and shut the door.

'Do be seated,' he said grandly, pointing to a low chair, wedged between the door and the desk. He took the swivel chair for himself and swung around in it like a demented little tycoon.

'Is this where you take on the mantle of Mr Arthur?'

He sniggered: 'No, he lives next door. This is my private Julian den. Don't worry, darling! I'm not going to bite you, even though you do look good enough to eat.'

Irritated by this skittishness, I said sharply: 'You kept very quiet about your Mr Arthur role. I always pictured you as one of life's butterflies.'

'And now you know the sordid truth? I suppose your friend Betty spilled the beans? Don't bother to deny it. I'm under no illusions about her, and it doesn't matter; I don't really mind your knowing.'

'Anyway, what's sordid about it? You should be proud of having such an important job. I'm sure we'd all have been madly impressed.'

He gave a neighing laugh: 'How naive can you get? You'd all have split your sides, I daresay, picturing me trudging off to work in a shop every morning.'

As it happened, I had been trudging off to my drama school every morning during the period in question, but I was so shattered by the depths of self-pity and misconception which his remarks revealed, that it did not seem worth mentioning. Luckily, Barnes tapped on the door and squeezed himself into the room, giving me a chance to recover my balance.

'Here we are, sir! One dry martini coming up, and champagne for the little lady!'

This avuncular manner rather took me aback, and, when he had gone, Julian said complacently: 'Quite a character, isn't he? I could see you were amused. It was a clever idea of mine, to put him in charge of our little bar, don't you agree?'

'Brilliant,' I replied, thinking there was something

vaguely off key about the question; but this was no new experience with Julian, and there was something else which puzzled me more.

'To go back to what you were saying, Julian: is it just because our paths don't cross now that you don't mind my knowing about your job here, or does the new image apply to everyone?'

'A shrewd question,' he replied, with another snort. 'And the answer is a bit of both. You and I are such old chums that I can let my hair down with you. And then, you see, my brother and I have built up something pretty important with this business. We have several branches outside London, too, you know. I'm no longer the humble shop assistant.'

'Oh, I'm sure they all pull the forelock, nowadays.'

'Ridicule was always your favourite weapon, wasn't it, Tessa? I can't say that marriage has improved you.'

'Whereas, you haven't given it a chance to?'

'Touché,' he replied, with a giggle.

I was halfway through my second glass of champagne, and I said: 'Well, do you intend to dance round the mulberry bush indefinitely, or have you really got something to show me?'

'Yes, indeed! Rather your line of country, too. It struck me, the minute you walked in here on Tuesday, that Fate must have sent you. See if you can guess what this is.'

He had stood up and was gingerly dislodging one of the folders from the top of the bookcase.

'No, I can't.'

'Aha! Another little secret of mine which no one guessed. You had no idea I kept a diary?'

'No, but a number of people do, and I am one of them. What's so special about it?'

'This is no ordinary diary, let me tell you.'

I could believe him. Having eased out the top folder, he placed it reverently on the desk. At a rough estimate, it contained about three hundred typed sheets.

'No, Tessa, my love, this is no ordinary diary. It's going to make a lot of people sit up and take notice. This is only the early part, mind you. The bulk of it is still in longhand. Are you impressed?'

'I find my reactions hard to describe, to be candid.'

'What would they be, if I offered to let you read it?'

'Even more indescribable,' I admitted, with a sinking heart.

'Well, I am. You see, Tessa, it's all there, every mood and detail of the period. And there are dozens of full-blooded characters, presented in the round, if you can understand me. Don't you see what a marvellous play it would make? It's got everything. It simply leaps out of the pages at you.'

I backed away nervously, in case it did so.

'And that was the miraculous thing about your turning up in my life again. Of course, I know what you're thinking: why me?'

'Yes, I am.'

'I'll explain. Naturally, I know dozens of theatrical people, a good deal more illustrious than you, if you don't mind my saying so, tee hee hee, but there's not one of them I could really trust. You're different, though. I do trust you, and I mean that, in spite of our little joke just now.'

'That's fine, but it doesn't mean I'm a playwright. My job is to speak whatever lines the author has seen fit to write down. Even that can be taxing enough.'

'Just so. It takes an actor to tell how a line will sound on the stage. That's why we'd make such a wonderful partnership. I'd do the creative work and you'd supply the technical know-how, as you people call it. What do you say?'

I could have said a lot, but he had spoken with such passionate sincerity that I dared not risk it. I flicked a corner of the manuscript: 'What's this, then, Julian, the prologue?'

'Should there be a prologue? I could easily write one in. This actually covers the first few years. It might need compressing a little, but that's where you come in. You'd know better than me what to cut out.'

For once, I agreed with him.

'Well, do at least say you'll read it. Please, Tessa darling!'

I found this last appeal even less attractive than his former bragging, but he had made it hard for me to refuse, and I reluctantly agreed. I warned him that I was a slow reader, which I fully intended to be, in this case.

Having gained his point, Julian wasted no more of his winning ways, and we arrived at the Savoy with hardly another word spoken. Even during lunch I was not required to give the ball of conversation anything more strenuous than an occasional pat, for he appeared to be acquainted with practically everyone in the room, and about half of them stopped at our table on their way in or out.

It recalled a phenomenon which had often struck me in the past; that he, who could have numbered his intimate friends on two fingers, had an acquaintance which ran into hundreds. They were not confined to headwaiters and their clients, either. I remembered how often he had been recognised by taxi-drivers, newspaper sellers and other normally anonymous people.

From the brief snatches of dialogue that were permitted to us, I learnt that Julian's family home in

Esher had been converted into three flats, for himself, his father, and his brother and sister-in-law. Also that this marriage had turned out badly. He even hinted that it was the calamitous example of Mr and Mrs Teddy which had dissuaded him from taking a wife of his own; thus driving an ocean liner through my theory that his bachelordom was simply due to there not being a woman in the land dotty enough to marry him.

My guess that the podgy man had been Brown Senior proved correct. I asked if he ruled them all with a rod of iron, and, after the usual interval for nodding and waving to far-flung corners of the room, Julian said: 'On the contrary. He's lost all interest in mundane affairs since my mother died.'

'So you and Teddy more or less run things?'

He glared at me, flushing angrily: 'I know you're not interested in vulgar commerce, Tessa, so please don't pretend. It doesn't cut any ice with me.'

Nor was any further reference made to the diary, until just as we were leaving, when he thrust the enormous folder into my hands: 'Guard it carefully. It's for your eyes alone. I'll let you have the rest as soon as I can get it typed.'

'How do you manage about that?' I asked idly. 'Is your typist a deaf mute, or is she another of those rare people that you trust?'

'I used to think so, indeed I did, but I'm beginning to wonder. She hasn't been near me for three weeks, and not one word. It's hideously worrying.'

'Do you suspect her of making a secret copy and hawking it round the theatre managements?'

'No, this is the only copy. I'd dearly like to know what she's up to, though.'

'Who is she?'

The commissionaire handed me into a taxi with the

lordly air of one who had personally fabricated it out of a pumpkin and six white mice. I wound down the window and leant forward, saying: 'Is she Jasmine Hawkes?'

The taxi jerked forward as I spoke, but there was time to see his expression. The complacent smirk had gone and his face looked pinched and frightened.

Four

'How was the money paid?' I asked Robin, voicing a thought which had been nagging at me all day, and his unhesitating response showed how heavily the blackmail case weighed on his mind:

'In one-pound notes, on a number twenty-five bus.'

'You're joking? Who did she give them to, the conductor?'

'No, she was told to go to Oxford Circus and board the first westbound twenty-five bus which stopped there, after five forty-five on a certain evening. She was to wear a white headscarf and to dump a brown suitcase containing the money in the cubby-hole under the stairs. She was then to go on top, and to leave the bus at the Green Park stop. What does all that suggest to you?'

'I don't know. What should it?'

'Well, consider the timing. You can see that the plan took maximum advantage of the rush hour, but, on the face of it, it was a remarkably haphazard arrangement. Let me begin in the best tradition by calling our victim Madam X ... and by the way, what shall we call the blackmailer? Y?'

'Oh, let's not, it's so confusing. Why not just plain B?'

'All right. So we assume that, by twenty to six, B is lined up in an adjacent queue at Oxford Circus, watching for X. The rush hour is not yet at its height, so he'll have no trouble in keeping her under observation. On the other hand, white headscarves aren't all that rare, so he must know her by sight, and she him, presumably. He'd have to keep in the background, but there'd have been too many people around for anyone to notice if he'd dropped back in the queue every time a bus drew up. Much the same applies to X. Her bus is unlikely to be so full as to prevent her getting a seat on top, but it would have been easy enough to shove the case in its hiding-place without even the conductor noticing.'

'Yes, I see.'

'But can't you see, too, how easily it could all go wrong? Presumably, as soon as B see X board her bus, he tries to follow her; but he's last in line, in that queue, and it's even chances that he'll be left behind. So what does that give us?'

'A very frustrated blackmailer, I should imagine.'

'No, I can't believe he wouldn't have taken such an eventuality into account. I'm convinced that this is where the accomplice comes in. What shall we call him? A for Accomplice, I suppose?'

'Yes, please.'

'And where would you have stationed A, if you'd been handling the operation?'

I thought it over and then said tentatively: 'How about the Green Park stop?'

Robin nodded: 'I agree. By keeping at the head of the queue there, A is a hundred per cent certain of boarding the bus as X leaves it. If B is already inside, so much the better. If not, all A has to do is to snatch the case when no one's watching, and get off at the next stop.'

'Simplicity itself!'

'Yes, and if it was worked like that, it tells us one very significant thing about A. He must have been someone that X wouldn't recognise. Unlike B, who could hover in the background, A is virtually bound to come face to face with X, as they get on and off the bus at the Green Park.'

'Which reminds me, Robin; didn't X have a shot at picking out B, herself? I'm sure I couldn't have resisted it?'

'The normal feminine reaction, in fact?'

'Oh well, it's always fatal to generalise about those, isn't it?'

'Apparently it is, for she insists that she acted purely mechanically, looking neither to left nor right. Her explanation is that the whole business was so revolting to her that she could only get through it by turning herself into a zombie, but I think there could be another reason, too, don't you?'

'Like having a theory about B's identity and scared to have it confirmed?'

'Possibly; and, if so, it shows that she privately believes B to be someone she knows reasonably well. Why else should she be so squeamish?'

'She will have to be a brave girl and face the truth, when Mr B is brought to trial,' I pointed out.

'Perhaps she isn't looking that far ahead. My impression is that she lives on the hope of a miracle, to make him chuck his hand in. She's evasive, though, and I don't believe for a moment that she's told us everything. Oh well, just have to press on, I suppose.'

This discussion, like others of its kind, took place in the privacy of our aperitif hour, and the subject was not reopened at dinner owing to the long ears of our little pitcher-server. Instead, I described my meeting with Julian and his friends, which, from Sebastian's point of view, was about the most spellbinding topic I could have chosen. When I got to the part about the diary, he became so carried away that he went on pouring wine into my glass long after it was full.

'And what have you done with this precious diary?' Robin asked, when Sebastian had scurried away to fetch a cloth. 'For God's sake, don't leave it lying around.'

'Don't worry; it's quite safe. Locked in the dressing-table drawer, with my best jewellery.'

'So all you have to remember now is where you put the key?'

'If it weren't for my jewellery, I'd rather the key was lost. The prospect of ploughing through someone else's intimate diary gives me the creeps.'

'All ship shape and Bristol fashion now,' Sebastian said, standing back to survey the smudges on the table. 'I'll get out the polishing kit and have a real going over in the morning.'

(ii)

To some extent, the morning was to find me similarly occupied.

It was probably inevitable that crime of every variety should loom large in my life, for Robin made a habit of mulling over the problems of his work when we were alone together. Friends, not similarly placed, were often startled by the casual way I attributed criminal intentions to perfectly harmless activities and found sinister implications in their most trivial remarks. But it was a specially odd coincidence that Robin should have been landed with an outsize blackmail case, within hours of my light-heartedly accusing Betty of the same activity. The connection was too nebulous to be worth mentioning, yet it was one which my superstitious nature could not wholly reject, and I believe it was then that I received the first intimations of there being some link between Robin's case and recent funny goings-on at Thurgoods.

The construction of the first vague outline of a plan for putting this theory to the test was interrupted by the arrival of Sebastian with my breakfast tray. He announced that, if it were all one to me, he would be taking the weekend off to flip over to Amsterdam.

Sebastian's Amsterdam trips occurred on an average of once a month, but I had no idea who paid for them, or why they were so important to him. As all my friendly pumping had met with dusty answers about having a bit of a tiptoe through the tulips, I had given up asking, but on this occasion it was far from being all one to me because we had invited forty or fifty people for supper on Sunday.

'Too bad it has to be this weekend,' I said craftily. 'You'll be missing a good party. Lots of theatre nobs.'

'Jes caint be helped, Ah guess, Miss Theresa, ma'am,' he replied, in his Southern mammy accent.

'You sound like a blue-haired old virago from Winnipeg, if it's any interest to you,' I said crossly.

'Ooh, aren't you awful?' he squealed, reverting to normal speech.

Awful or not, I was powerless to dissuade him.

The next impediment to constructive thought was a telephone call from my cousin Toby, to ask if we could put him up on Sunday night. He was a playwright by profession, and a recluse by inclination and could only rarely be enticed out of his country retreat, but it transpired that he had been summoned by the officials of the Inland Revenue Department to appear before them at eleven o'clock on Monday morning. Being a late riser, or, to put it another way, bone idle, he was prepared to pay the supreme sacrifice of spending a night in London.

Robin and I doted on Toby, but he could hardly have picked a more unfavourable day for his visit. To forestall future recriminations, I pitched it strong: 'I must warn you that there will be approximately four thousand people here on Sunday evening.'

'Oh, God! Can't you put them off?'

'There isn't time, and they would be so disappointed.'

'You flatter yourself. I should think most of them would see it as a merciful reprieve. I know I should.'

'Which is one reason why I didn't invite you. Come to that why not postpone your interview until Tuesday? One more day couldn't make your plight any worse.'

'Yes, it could. I've broken the last ten appointments, and now they've thrown down the gauntlet.'

'Well, I don't see any help for it. You will just have to suffer one evening among civilised people for once in your life.'

'Perhaps I could have dinner upstairs on a tray? That wouldn't overstrain the resources, would it? I shall need a quiet period to go through all these threatening letters.'

'Don't you have an accountant for this sort of thing?'

'I used to, but he died. Jumped out of a window in Throgmorton Street. Looking at this lot, one does see why.'

An idea for his salvation had come into my head, but I decided not to raise hopes prematurely, and told him to arrive in time for tea, so that we could have a peaceful pow-wow, before the invasion started.

He agreed to this and, when he had rung off, I lifted the telephone again and dialled an Ealing number.

'Hallo!' I said, 'How are you, and how's Bobs?'

The preliminaries over, matters went forward in a satisfactory fashion, and afterwards, swept along by a rare and heady sense of purpose, I resolved to polish up the shining hour to a positive dazzle by embarking on Julian's diary. Twenty minutes was the period I allotted myself for this chore, which I estimated as ample for skimming through the first forty or fifty pages.

I found the key of my dressing-table drawer without much difficulty, only twenty-four hours having elapsed since I had put it away in its new hiding-place, a gold evening bag which I hardly ever used.

Some of my resolution melted away as I lifted out the bulky mass. I told myself that, after all, ten minutes would do very well, for a start. Two hours later I was still poring over it, goggle-eyed and appalled.

It opened, innocuously enough, with a description of our hero's twenty-first birthday. The occasion had been notable for the fact that he had fulfilled a long-felt desire to adopt the name of Julian, finding it more suited to his looks and personality than the one he had received at birth, and a more appropriate label with which to break into the world he aspired to above all others, and which he called Society with a capital S.

Nor had familiarity dulled the name's appeal, for he referred to himself throughout in the third person. Perhaps this device enabled him to romanticise himself more thoroughly, and certainly it required a constant effort to reconcile the suave and glamorous Julian of the narrative with the blustering old fuss budget that I knew in real life. The rest of the cast were referred to only by initials, or nicknames of his own invention. The advantages of this, if not the reason, soon became clear.

At first, Julian had been diligent in keeping daily records of every trivial event, from which a picture slowly emerged of his attitude to the other members of his family; namely that he detested his father and despised his younger brother. The only one for whom he had a genuine affection was his mother, and she had been a chronic invalid from the opening page until her death, some two years later.

So far as I could piece it together Barnes had been the prop and mainstay of Mrs Brown and Julian during this period. He had been promoted from his job as gardener/handyman, to attend on the ailing woman, and, with endless devotion and patience, had gradually become indispensable to her.

Mr Brown had strongly disapproved of Barnes's monopoly, thereby earning himself another black mark, but had been powerless to interfere. Mrs Brown, from whom Julian had evidently inherited his obsession about the superiority of trustworthiness over all other virtues, had retained an unshakeable faith in Barnes right up to her death. Neither the deterioration in her condition, nor the frequent and painful attacks she suffered would induce her to have a nurse. She had been supported in this stand by her elder son, and never more resolutely than when Mr Brown had made a feeble attempt to introduce a candidate of his own to take over Barnes's duties. This was one L.B., a young woman, distantly related, and with some previous nursing experience. However, Julian had nothing but contempt for her looks and breeding and had scarcely allowed her inside his mother's bedroom.

All this, naturally, widened still farther the gap between the two factions, and, during Mrs Brown's last hours, only Julian and Barnes had been present at her bedside. Very likely, the poor creature had suffered from some incurable abdominal disease, and her life would not have been much prolonged, even by expert nursing. I judged that it must have been so, otherwise her doctor would not have signed the death certificate; and perhaps, in these circumstances, it would be better to die among people one loved and trusted. Nevertheless, it was faintly unnerving to discover that Julian had not evinced one shred of remorse for his own conduct. As the entries piled up, it became impossible not to suspect that his grief had been mitigated by the acquisition of a large income.

On his mother's death, he had gained control of a sizeable fortune, which had been left in trust by his maternal grandfather. This was the original Thurgood, the founder, among other successful enterprises, of the firm which bore his name. The only condition of the legacy was that he should become a full-time employee at the shop, working his way up, in the good old tradition, from the basement.

He had swallowed this pill in the jam with fair grace, but the true purpose of his life had become even more firmly fixed on ascending the social ladder, and the diary, at this stage, was filled with grandiose schemes for laying out the money in a manner best calculated to raise him in the eyes of his beloved Society.

Up to that point, it had made mildly interesting reading, in a macabre sort of way, but a little later on things took an uglier turn. Perhaps if his new wealth had opened more of the doors he so longed to enter he would have strutted cheerfully on through life, getting a great kick out of seeing himself through rose-coloured glasses and doing no damage to anyone. Unfortunately, a succession of snubs had curdled the milk of human kindness and turned him from a harmless lunatic into a ragingly embittered one. Every ounce of energy and enthusiasm turned towards revenging himself on those who had slighted him. Vindictiveness was the new absorption, and no stone was too small or too dirty to be turned over, in his relentless search for scandalous or discreditable information.

All this naturally became tedious and repellent after a while. The use of initials made his subjects hard to identify, even if there had been any special inducement to try. Nevertheless, some faint whiffs of ancient scandals, which I had heard my elders discussing, came wafting back down the years. One of these, in a particularly revolting passage, related to a family which no amount of pseudonyms could prevent my recognising as former friends of my parents. The climax of the story, as reported by Julian, had been the suicide of a prominent public figure, but my nurse had been friendly with the governess of the household, and some scraps of background gossip had filtered through to my eager childish mind. Time had not obliterated them, either, because my nurse had told me that this governess was the daughter of aristocratic parents who had fallen on hard times; a romantic, though probably fallacious history, which had greatly appealed to me at the time.

Thereafter, the journal appeared to me in a more sinister light. Morbid curiosity might have kept me glued until the last page, but the temptation was withheld. A series of piercing screams from Sebastian shot me back into blessed reality.

'What now?' I asked in a dazed voice, as his distraught face appeared round the door.

It transpired that his passport was out of date.

'Expired yesterday, if you please,' he moaned. 'Oh, I could kill myself, I really could.'

'That settles it,' I told him. 'You can't possibly get

it renewed in time. It takes at least five days.'

'Oh, I don't need a real passport, not for Holland and those places. I can get one of those temporary jobs from the post office. Bit of a come down, but there you are!'

'Why all the fuss, then?'

'Well, you've got to produce three passport photos, you see. Look, would you mind terribly if I slipped out and got some done? There's a place down the Strand where they do them while you wait.'

'I think I can spare you,' I said graciously.

'You didn't need me here, to listen for the phone?'

'No, I'll be here, myself; I've got a script to read.'

'Oh, ta ever so much. I'll just rush up and change into something a bit decent, and nip off there straight away. I'll be back in time to help with the dinner.'

Once he had gone and the thread snapped, I found a positive aversion to reading any more of the diary, and I thankfully put the manuscript away and locked the drawer. I debated for a while about a new hiding-place for the key, before deciding that the old one had not yet outlived its span, and replaced it in the gold bag.

For all his protestations, Sebastian did not return until after seven. He was coy about showing me the photographs, and I was not sufficiently interested to press the point. Perhaps he was disappointed by my indifference, for he took an envelope from his wallet and thrust it ostentatiously into the kitchen dresser drawer. I made a mental note to take a peek at it, while he was in Holland, but, unluckily for us both, I completely forgot.

Five

With Sebastian away for the weekend, I had to devote myself exclusively to preparations for the party, and there was no opportunity to glance again at Julian's diary.

Our male guests already outnumbered the women and the addition of Toby further upset the balance, so on a last-minute impulse I invited Betty. She and Toby were old friends and I knew that her presence would do much to reconcile him to the torments of the evening.

We lunched out on Sunday and made a leisurely detour home through St James's Park. When we turned into Beacon Square we saw Toby's green Mercedes parked outside the house. He was sitting at the wheel, his terrible old hat pulled down over his eyes, and looking very put upon.

'No one at home,' he complained. 'And no key under the mat. What sort of a welcome is that?'

'A thousand pardons,' I said, 'but we have to be extra careful about locking up in this establishment.'

'Yes, I suppose there would be rather a loss of face, if you were burgled, but what about the dreaded Twinkletoes? Do you have to lock him up, too?'

'He's in Holland.'

'What a relief! Your telephone has been ringing, by the way.'

I did not go into my usual spin because it was Sunday, and anyway my agent was coming to the party. For once, it was Robin who sped to the telephone.

A few minutes later, he came into the kitchen, where Toby was watching me make the tea, to say that he was needed at his office. He apologised for deserting me and promised to try and be home before the balloon went up.

The mention of offices had a bad effect on Toby, who became very glum over the prospect of his forthcoming ordeal.

'Don't worry,' I told him. 'I've fixed the whole thing, and your troubles are practically over.'

I perceived a certain incredulity in his expression, so gave him a thumbnail sketch of Sandy and her miraculous powers, adding that she would arrive at eight o'clock the following morning, to prepare his defence at the interview.

'It was terrific luck getting her,' I went on. 'Normally, on Monday, she goes to Mrs Haynes with the home-made fudge, but I remembered that relations there were rather strained. So I rang her up and Lo! Mrs Haynes has been told where she gets off, and Sandy is free to sort out your fiscal affairs.'

'I know you mean well, Tessa, but I'm not sure that a career in home-made fudge is quite the answer. I admit that my affairs are in something of a tangle, but to describe them in that way is rather overstepping the mark.'

So I had to launch into another invigorating pep talk, and he seemed partially convinced, although now beginning to whine about having to be up so early in the morning.

'No need for that,' I assured him. 'Sandy has her own keys, so just leave the papers on my desk and she'll do the rest.'

It was a plan after his own heart and he acquiesced without more demur; which was just as well, for time was galloping by and I had enough on my hands, without demurs to cope with as well.

(ii)

There were two or three curry dishes on the evening's menu and, to harmonise with this theme, I wore a new white and gold trouser suit, which had been made from an Indian sari. It had a matching scarf, which was intended to be casually knotted at the neck and I possessed just the right exotic, oriental brooch to keep the casual effect intact. Unfortunately, it was not to be found among the best jewellery and I concluded that, in a fit of *folie de grandeur*, I had hidden it in the second-best cache. However, before I could recollect where this was, the doorbell rang and I had to go down and let in the first arrivals.

A dozen more, including Betty, had been added to their number before I saw Robin go scurrying through the hall, and upstairs, three steps at a time. Estimating that he would need only a few minutes, I went to fetch the first consignment from the oven. I carried it back into the dining-room, whose double doors into the drawing-room had been opened, to make a large L-shaped room, and set the dishes out on the table. I had my back to the archway between the rooms, and Betty and Toby were standing nearby, talking about their glorious childhood adventures, when Betty abruptly broke off these nostalgic reminiscences and said: 'What's that man doing here?'

'Which man?'

'Tall fair one, who's just come in.'

'I expect Tessa invited him; he's her husband.'

'You're not serious?'

'Yes, I am. His name is Robin Price and he is

married to Tessa. Anything else you want to know?'

I hoped there would be, for it is always fascinating to overhear remarks about oneself, however uninformative, but Betty may have become aware of my presence for she moved away, and at the same moment my agent bounded up to ask if I would consider a Sunday night performance with some gallant little company who were staging a series of controversial plays in a disused warehouse.

It would have been unfair to accused my agent of mixing business with pleasure, because business is her main pleasure in life. Since there was not the slightest chance of shaking her off, I asked her to accompany me to the kitchen, where I would lend an ear to her proposals.

When we returned to the fray, I found that Toby had been collared by our guest of honour, a frail-looking nonagenarian, whose current play, in which she gave eight performances a week, had been running for over a year. There was no sign of Betty and no one could tell me what had become of her. I finally ran her to earth in my bedroom, where she was huddled over the dressing-table, staring at her own reflection in the glass. There was a cigarette burning down in the ashtray, so I concluded that she was not seriously indisposed, and I said: 'Anything wrong?'

'Yes. I don't know what you put in that curry thing, but I had one mouthful and it practically blew my head off.'

'Oh, sorry, Betty. The prawns are rather piquant, I admit. Robin was supposed to warn everyone. Shall I bring you something else?'

'No, don't fuss. Just leave me alone for a bit, and I'll be all right.'

I went slowly downstairs, worried by this new

development. I could not quite swallow the idea that biting on a hot chilli could knock out such a robust old campaigner as Betty, and I became obsessed with the idea that, in my brief off-stage period, Robin had inadvertently said something to upset her. I edged my way towards him, but was intercepted by the guest of honour, who commanded me to stop thrashing about like a fretful sheepdog, and to come and sit down.

'Pretty little fancy dress, Deeah,' she said, gazing with luminous, tragic eyes at my Indian suit, 'but you should remember not to fidget when you're wearing it. Repose is the great thing. Orientals understand it so well. Repohse, deeah, Repohse,' she continued, in a kind of chant.

She boomed on in this strain for several minutes, relating how she had reposed herself in all five continents, and in other circumstances, I should have been happy to have listened all night to her wit and wisdom, but part of my mind remained obstinately on what she called the fidget. However, as she was literally the most formidable old Dame in show business, it behoved me not to betray my impatience. So I crossed my ankles and exuded rapt and reposeful attention to every word. When she was bored with this, she emitted a peal of silvery laughter, which turned every head in our direction, and a godlike young film actor, named Peter Hitchens, stepped forward, dead on cue, and took my place.

A second trip in search of Betty proved even more futile. She had gone and there was a note on the dressing-table: 'Sorry, Tess, but I feel a bit groggy. See you some time. B.'

I applied some fresh make up to the face of the fretful sheepdog and went slowly back to my guests;

but my heart was no longer in it, and I could hardly wait for them to leave.

'You should be flushed with success,' Toby said, when the longed-for moment arrived. 'But, I must say, you look wizened.'

'I feel it,' I replied. 'It's too much damned hard work, on top of all the cooking. And what's it all for? Where are the pressures and tensions of modern life leading us? Just tell me that.'

'They are leading me straight to bed, if you really want to know,' Robin said, yawning. 'I am one of those non-housewives who have to get up in the morning.'

'So am I,' Toby admitted, looking rather wizened, himself, at the thought of it.

'If you take my advice,' Robin said, holding out an arm for me to lean on, 'you'll do the same, and leave all the clearing up for Sebastian.'

'Not a bad idea, but what about Sandy?'

'Oh, she can let herself in and I'll take her some coffee. I'll bring you some, too, if you promise not to get up.'

'What an angel you are!' I murmured, as we toiled upstairs for the last time. I meant it, too, and it was such a relief not to have quarrelled with him over Betty.

Six

'It's nine o'clock, Tessa. Sandy's here. She says your cousin must be an awful chump to have got himself into such a pickle, but she'll soon have him tickety boo.'

'Good old Sandy,' I said drowsily. 'Won't it be lovely to see Toby, when he's tickety boo?'

'Don't be tempted to get up for it.'

'No, I don't mean to raise a finger.'

In saying this, I had reckoned without Julian. His voice came bleating down the telephone ten minutes after Robin left, and it was as well that the coffee had cleared my head, for he began by saying:

'Come on! What do you think of my *oeuvre*?'

'Not bad, if you happen to be fond of dynamite.'

'Ah! Have you finished it?'

'Not quite.'

'Still, you must have formed some opinion, by now. What are the chances of its making a play? Tell me the worst.'

As usual, his twitching sensitivity brought out the moral coward in me, and instead of giving it to him straight from the shoulder, I said: 'To start with, there are too many characters, and not enough plot.'

'Plot? What nonsense! It's picaresque, can't you understand? A sort of modern Don Quixote, one might say.'

I had feared one might, and was ready for it.

'With the difference that you are alive and so are most of your characters. However much you changed the names, a lot of them would be recognisable. Even I recognised a few. There'd be libel actions galore.'

'No one would dare. It would be tantamount to admitting the truth of what I've said. You must be very naive not to see that.'

I did not dispute this for it was not worth the trouble. My intention was simply to find out what I could about Jasmine Hawkes, and I knew I should fail in it if I antagonised him.

'Well, I might come up with something a bit more constructive later on, but you say the rest isn't typed yet?'

'You haven't been particularly flattering about it, so far. I am not sure I should let you read the rest.'

'Please yourself.'

'Now, darling, don't get snooty. That was only my joke.'

It was not always easy to tell, in these dialogues with Julian, which of us was the cat and which the mouse, but, snatching the former role for myself whenever it offered, I said: 'I'm only doing my best to advise you.'

'I know, and I do depend on you, Tessa. The problem is, it's not typed, as you say, and I'm told my handwriting is difficult.'

'Well, what about your Miss Hawkes? Has she really left? I presume she was the one?'

'Yes, she was. I suppose Betty Haverstock put you on to that. I wish she'd mind her own damn business.'

'I don't know why you employed poor Betty, if you dislike her so much.'

'I didn't employ her, dammit. My father did: and over my head, too. He met her at some charity thing and fell for those raddled charms hook, line and sinker.'

'Also she happens to be an expert on antiques, as I suppose he was shrewd enough to discover?'

'You suppose wrong, then, because it had nothing to do with it. She wormed her way in by pretending to be dead keen on this spiritualist racket.'

'Anyway, that's not the point. I was asking why your Miss Hawkes had left.'

'Frankly, Tessa, it's a complete mystery. She was another like yourself that I'd known for ever so long and trusted implicitly. I never dreamt of her working for me, until a few months ago. Then I discovered that she and her mother were fearfully hard up and that she was doing a bit of secretarial work. It was like the answer to a prayer; except that three weeks ago she vanished into the blue.'

'And you've no idea where?'

'Oh yes, I have. I heard from her on Saturday. She coolly said that she'd been ill and had gone to the country.'

'So what's all the fuss about? She'll be back soon, no doubt.'

'Wrong again, Miss Clever. She had the nerve to say that she and her mother had bought some hotel outside Stratford. A likely tale!'

'It's been done before.'

'Not without capital, and she gave me to understand they were on their beam ends. No, she just didn't like the work and hadn't the guts to say so. Now, I simply don't know where to turn.'

I said cautiously: 'As it happens, I do know someone who's an absolute marvel at that kind of work. I might be able to persuade her to take you on.'

'Oh, that wouldn't do at all,' he said irritably. 'I could never work with a stranger, someone I wasn't in perfect harmony with.'

'Don't be goofy, Julian. Can't you see that's the very type to avoid. I've already told you that I identified several of your characters, and I'm sure some of your contemporaries would pick out a lot more. It could land you in frightful complications. But this friend of mine is different. Even if she did see through some of your aliases, it would never occur to her to pass it on. Can't you see the advantages?'

'You're very persuasive, Tessa, but the idea of a stranger prying into ... Well, to be honest, it goes against the grain.'

'Then it's your silly old grain that's at fault. Think it over and let me know, if you change your mind.'

'Yes, I will, but I'd like to talk it over first. How about today? I'll give you lunch, if you're a good girl.'

The prospect of another session with him was not alluring, specially on such patronising terms; but the havoc downstairs was even less inviting, and I settled for a drink in the Boardroom, at twelve-thirty. A further inducement was the chance this would provide for passing on to Betty the good news about Jasmine Hawkes, and perhaps of getting to the bottom of her strange behaviour at the party.

I put the telephone down and dozed off again, but seemed hardly to have closed my eyes when the door opened and Sandy's head appeared:

'My, you look comfy! Snug as the proverbial bug. Hope I didn't disturb your dreams?'

'What's the time?'

'Half past ten, and we're just off.'

'Like lambs to the slaughter, poor you!'

'Not to worry. Everything's under control. Poor Mr Crichton's in a fearful flap, but I've told him there's no need for panic stations. They can't hang him, and I mean to tear a few strips off the blighters. Your henchman is back, by the way.'

'That's good. Not that he does much henching, as

you know. Give him my regards and say I expect to find everything extremely Bristol fashion, by the time I come down.'

'Will do. Ta-ta for now, then.'

'Tatty-bye, Sandy darling.'

After this, even an amateur in the laws of probability could have foreseen that I had only to close my eyes for Sebastian to come thundering on the door; so, with only two hours to spare, I applied myself once more to Julian's diary. I knew that a great burden would be lifted, if I could get to the end and return it to him with a clear conscience; for, the longer it remained in my custody, the more uneasy I became about this explosive material falling into the wrong hands.

This task proved to be quite as tedious and depressing as I had anticipated, but at least it provided nothing to harrow in a personal sense. The closing pages were devoted exclusively to a detailed account of the trial and conviction of someone he called 'Mason'. This character, whose real name was not divulged, had been at school with Julian and had incurred his dislike by outstripping him both in games and work. Julian had waited twelve years for his revenge, and had got it by sitting unobtrusively in the back of the courtroom listening to his old rival being sent down for three years, for fraud and embezzlement.

I closed the folder, vowing that, typed or untyped, I would never be coerced into reading another disgusting word.

Seven

I paused at the first floor, but only for two minutes because Betty was not there. Her assistant explained that she was visiting a client in the country.

She had not been expecting me and I knew that she often gave people professional advice about interior decorating and so on, yet this continued elusiveness revived all my misgivings. Everything in her behaviour over the past few days had justified Robin's censure, and was so violently at odds with the frank, straightforward person I believed her to be.

I remained standing in the lift when it reached the second floor, trying to talk myself out of a profound uneasiness, until metaphorically brought back to earth by a fusillade of bangs on the outer door and a familiar voice shouting: 'What's wrong with this blasted lift? Get on and open the door, can't you?'

Realising that the outer door remained locked so long as there was a passenger inside, I obediently drew back the grille, to be confronted by Mrs Teddy in a most uncertain mood.

Her face was an even brighter pink than usual and, with her beaky nose and pale, wispy hair, the effect was distressingly blotchy and unbecoming.

'Oh, at last!' she squawked, on a note of screaming exasperation; then, peering at me with near-sighted eyes, dropped her voice an octave or two: 'Beg pardon, I didn't see it was a customer. Thought you were one of the staff.'

'That would explain everything,' I agreed.

'All the same, you've no business up here, you know. This is a private room, and admission is by invitation only.'

'I have an appointment with Mr Julian Brown.'

'Oh! Oh well, my apologies for keeping you,' she muttered, pushing past me into the lift.

Except for Barnes, the room was deserted, and I was skirting the long table and heading for the end door, when he called out: 'Shouldn't, if I were you, madam.'

'Shouldn't what?' I demanded. It was the second time in as many minutes that I had been addressed in peremptory terms by a member of the Thurgood establishment, and it was making me jumpy.

'Go in that office, that's what. Not if you was to take my advice.'

'But Mr Julian is expecting me.'

'That may well be, madam, but just now he's in conference, if you like to call it that. More of a ding dong, by the sound of it; and Mrs Teddy just come flying out with her tail up, as I fancy you had occasion to notice. How about a drop, while you're waiting? Champagne, isn't it?'

I had felt mildly curious about Barnes, since reading part of his life story in the diary, and I seated myself at his little bar saying: 'The driest you have, please.'

He had the midday edition, opened at the racing page and spread out over the bar. There was a notepad beside it, on which he had evidently been jotting down some calculations.

'Any hot tips for this afternoon?' I inquired.

'There's Hippie Girl in the four o'clock, as I rather fancy. Came second at Newbury, and the going should suit her better today.'

'You're quite an expert, I gather?'

'I have my ups and downs. Do you follow it yourself?'

'I enjoy going to meetings, but off the course betting doesn't have the same fascination.'

'There now! And, with me, it's the reverse. You'll hardly credit this, madam, but I've never been on a race-course in my life. Studied form and all that for donkey's years, but never seen it in the flesh, as you might say.'

'Gracious!' I said, rather stuck for a suitable comment on what he evidently considered to be the all-time, world sensation. 'You should try it some time.'

'Don't fancy it, somehow. No interest in horses, as such, if you follow me, and I can't say I like crowds, either.'

'Is that what appeals to you about this job?'

'Come again,' he said, jerking round suspiciously.

'I wondered why an experienced person like yourself should take a job here, where you can't get much opportunity to use your skills. I suppose it gives you time to follow your hobby?'

'Very perspicacious of you, madam, if you'll permit me to say so. There are some, who'd been in my shoes, as'd go bonkers, I daresay, cooped up here best part of the day.'

'Yes, you don't seem to get many customers, but I suppose things are a bit more lively during the Board Meetings?'

'Yes and no, like,' he said mysteriously. 'Still, it's not all play and no work, you know. I'm in charge of all the cleaning on this floor, too. Very time-consuming it can be, with all the glass and that.'

'And those two rooms are the other Directors' offices, are they?' I asked, nodding at the two doors nearest the lift.

'Oh no, madam, not any more. Mr and Mrs Teddy are on the ground floor, and the old gentleman has an office off the antiques. Those two, to which you are referring, they used to be secretaries' rooms, but Mr Julian had them turned into cloakrooms, when this bar was put in. One each for the ladies and gentlemen. Not much cleaning needed there, though, the amount they're used. Oh yes, it can be very monotonous at times, but it suits me. I'm by way of being a recluse, if you take my meaning?'

I took it all right, but before I could give expression to any further perspicacities on the subject, the door of Julian's office swung open. Though still out of vision, I heard him say, in his most tight-strung voice: 'Oh, Barnes, when Mrs Price arrives, please ask her . . .'

'Here already, sir. Just having a pick-me-up till you was disengaged.'

He shot through the door and bustled towards me: 'Oh, darlingest Tessa, do forgive me. Something cropped up which I simply had to deal with, but don't go, my angel, will you?'

Contrary to expectations, the greeting and the feverish glint in his eye indicated the utmost good humour. Presumably, the ding-dong was going in his favour.

I consented to wait a few more minutes and he disappeared behind the arras again. This time the door remained open and I could distinguish two other voices. Then out shambled old Mr Brown, with a pale, distraught Mr Teddy flapping along behind. They stood together, waiting for the lift to come up, glancing neither at us nor each other.

Barnes watched them sardonically and, when they had gone, set my glass on a tray and led the way to Julian's office.

The atmosphere of the tiny room was clogged with stale cigar smoke, and, since neither this nor Julian's high-pitched mood was particularly inviting, I said firmly: 'I came to return your diary, but I've got a lunch date and I can't stop.'

'Yes, I know all that, but I must talk to you. Do you know what that discussion was about? You'd never guess in a million years.'

I had been trained in answering far less leading questions than this, however, and asked if it had anything to do with his diary.

He looked so enraptured that I thought I was in for more praises for my perspicacity, but, in fact, he said: 'What you couldn't guess is that my sister-in-law has been creeping up here on the quiet and nosing through my papers. How do you like that?'

'Words fail me.'

'Yes,' he said complacently, 'I thought they would. Now, perhaps, people will believe me when I tell them what a deceitful slut she is.'

'How did you find out?'

'My darling girl, she made no secret of it. She pretended to be very concerned about the family reputation, if an outsider should get hold of it; and you know what? She says I'm unbalanced and in need of psychiatric treatment. Did you ever hear of anything so fantastic?'

Luckily, the question was rhetorical, but I was puzzled by his reactions. I would have expected his persecution mania to be at its liveliest in this crisis, but his elation increased with every word.

'Why the sudden panic? They must have known you kept a diary?'

'Yes, but no one has ever read it. It was when she heard it was being typed that she became so inquisitive.

Now, who can have told her that? Do you suppose your friend Betty was responsible?'

'Most unlikely. She has no more time for your sister-in-law than you have.'

'So we're left with only one culprit?'

'Jasmine, herself?'

'Precisely. It was to have been a dead secret between the two of us, and I trusted her implicitly; but she's betrayed me all along the line. She'll live to regret that. I'll pay her out, if it's the last thing I do.'

Remembering my promise to Betty, I said: 'Have you kept her letter, Julian?'

'Naturally. I want to be reminded of her treachery.'

'May I see it? I've got a theory,' I said, improvising at full tilt. 'And I want to test it.'

'Oh, by all means read it, in that case. I find this most intriguing.'

He took an envelope from one of the desk drawers and handed it over. The name and address were typed and it contained a single sheet of paper, whose message I already knew. There was no date or address, and it was signed 'Birdie'.

'Birdie?'

'Oh, it was my special name for her in the old days. Jasmine became Jay, and Jay became Birdie. Got it? Never mind about that. Tell me, have you proved your theory?'

'I'm afraid this is inconclusive,' I said truthfully, as I handed the letter back.

'Now you've got me on tenterhooks. What can you be driving at?'

I had purposely wrapped my request in layers of ambiguity, believing this to be the surest way of gaining his co-operation, so I put on an enigmatic expression and said that Only Time Would Tell, etcetera, and he looked more enchanted than ever.

'As for the other upset,' I said, when I felt that enough wool covered his eyes, 'I suppose it will blow over?'

'Ha! That shows you don't know Lavender. She never lets go, once she's got her teeth in. Though she may have bitten off more than she can chew this time, tee, hee, hee.'

I lost the drift at this point, and Julian's monologue rambled on unheeded. I interrupted it to ask: 'Was her maiden name Bagge, by any chance?'

'Who? Lavender? Of course not, and do pay attention. This is desperately serious and there isn't a moment to lose. I shall have the lock changed on this door, but that won't keep her out for long; so I've got to take counter-measures, but I'll come to that in a moment. First of all, about this typist you recommended: What proof have I that she's trustworthy?'

'All I can tell you is that Robin and I rely on her completely, and she is engaged at this minute on secret and confidential work for my cousin, Toby Crichton.'

'Oh, he's your cousin, is he? Well, well, that might be useful. You must introduce me. Well, that sounds all right. Give me her name and telephone number and I'll see if she can start tomorrow.'

'You'll do no such thing,' I said sternly.

'Why ever not?'

'In the first place, she could only give you one day a week and you wouldn't stand a chance with that approach. She's very choosy about who she works for, and, believe me, she can afford to be. I'll do my best for you, but the earliest she could start would be next Monday.'

'But that's a whole week away; that's no good at all. I've been trying to impress you with the urgency of all this and you calmly talk about next Monday. Don't you see that the only way to foil Lavender is to get several copies typed immediately, and hide them in different places? This is my life's work and I'm not going to stand by and watch her destroy it. It's no use taking it home, because she's bound to have a key to my flat, and I can't stand guard here for twenty-four hours a day. Now do you understand?'

'I understand it from your point of view, but it doesn't alter mine. Either we do it my way, or it's off.'

He brought out every threat and blandishment in his repertoire, but I would not budge. Self interest was mainly responsible for my efforts to obtain a Monday job for Sandy, over which I could retain some control; but I knew him to be capable of so effectually antagonising her, at the outset, that she would swim rapidly away, not only out of his ken but Robin's and mine, too.

He capitulated at last, but there is always a price for such victories, and faint remorse for having won the battle, combined with his crestfallen looks, undermined my resistance to the next demand. This was a trifling request to have the diary delivered to Beacon Square that very evening. It was no surprise to learn that this course had been decided upon because he trusted me.

'I know that,' I moaned. 'And I do wish you didn't.'

'You should feel flattered, my dear girl. There aren't many of whom I could say it. I've been let down too often. Besides, I'm only asking you to give house-room to one small suitcase. Pack it away with your fur coats, or something, and we'll take out one section at a time, for this secretary to work on. That should be simple enough.'

'Supposing Lavender found out? She might come

and burn the house down, and Robin would never forgive me. I bet her spies are everywhere. How about Barnes, for one?'

'Oh, nonsense! I've known Barnes since I was a child. He's a real character, and I trust him implicitly.'

The sequitur struck me as distinctly non, but it was pointless to argue, so I said: 'If you must bring it, it had better be on Wednesday evening. San ... this secretary will be there, and I'll be able to sound her out, in advance. You could meet, sort of casually, and see how you hit it off.'

'I must say, you handle her with kid gloves, don't you, Tessa? One has the impression of a very sensitive plant.'

'One would do well to keep that impression,' I told him.

So the compromise was reached. I consented to take charge of the suitcase, and he to leave the handling of Sandy to me. I undertook my part against my better judgement, but it was not until later that I realised how much better my better judgement would have been.

(ii)

If proof of Sandy's superhuman powers had still been lacking, it was to be found, three hours later, in the cheerfulness which had broken in on Toby.

He was dashing away at the *Times* crossword without a care in the world, and actually complimented me on the way I had trained Tippety Toes to make decent China tea.

'Am I to take it that things are now tickety boo?'

'Well on the road to tickety. Your Miss Pheno Barbitone seems to have friends in high places.'

'Phelps Sanderson. I suppose she had them all eating out of her hand?'

'Including the Lord Chief Puss-in-Boots, himself. I should hang on to her, if I were you.'

'I mean to, although we tread a perilous path. Anyway, it was thoughtful of you to wait and tell me. I rather expected you to be haring back to the country by now.'

'I think of staying an extra night. The idea was to escort you both to a play. Unless you would prefer some other small token of my gratitude?'

'No, a play is just the token I would choose, but can you afford it? What about all this retrenchment and so forth, which you've doubtless had preached at you this morning?'

'Not so. I must say, it was an eye opener to me. There I was, dining on cornflakes and switching the lights off at nine o'clock, and I should have been throwing my money around and charging everything to expenses. That way solvency lies, believe it or not.'

'I'd believe anything, but I can't quite see how you can charge Robin and me to expenses.'

'Oh, easily. We'll say I'm writing a script for you and you have to be coaxed along with little treats. Singleton Bates will rig the whole thing. In fact, if we could get the house seats and take my car, it wouldn't surprise me if we not only broke even, but actually made a profit.'

It sounded like a practical scheme and we set to work to find a play which was doing rotten business and where the parking amenities measured up to requirements.

Robin came in when we had narrowed the choice to three, so we gave him the casting vote, and Toby went off to telephone some influential quarters.

'Had a good day?' I asked.

'No. Rather foul, really.'

'Oh, Robin, what a shame! But it's fun having Toby here, isn't it? All the same, I rather wish he wasn't.'

'You're not making sense.'

'Well, you didn't get much sleep last night and you look a bit down. You might have preferred a quiet evening on our own?'

'Oh no, only halfway down, and that's because I'm operating in a kind of void. Inaction is the real horror, so it's probably just as well we are going out. Does that make you feel better?'

'Much better,' I agreed, wondering for the umpteenth time what I had ever done to deserve him.

Sadly enough, however, Toby's first excursion into higher economics was not a success. It was a play of such stultifying boredom that he was obliged to plunge most of his profits on stiff drinks for the interval. Nevertheless, Robin had caught the bug by this time, and insisted on saving some money, too, by taking us out to supper. So it was past midnight before I had an opportunity to revert to the subject of Mr B, and was by then almost too sleepy to take in the answers.

'What has happened,' I asked, 'to create this void of yours?'

'Nothing; that's the trouble. He has vanished down a hole in the ground.'

I suggested, with a smothering yawn, that this might be the best place for him.

'Yes, but there are snags. In the first place, he'll doubtless bob up again when it suits him; and we still don't know his identity. If word of his activities were to reach us in the future, we'd have to start all over again from scratch. But the real question is: who tipped him off?'

'You think it might have been Madam X, herself?'

'Not intentionally, perhaps. It's more likely that she disobeyed orders and confided in one other person, about the trap we'd laid for him, mistakenly believing him or her to be safe.'

'That should make things easier for you,' I mumbled. 'All you have to do is put her closest friends under the microscope and see which one of them reveals the fatal flaw of being teamed up with a bunch of blackmailers.'

Even as I uttered them, these words struck some hitherto silent chord in my subconscious with an echoing twang, and I could hardly wait for a fresh new day to come and enable me to put my own sound advice into practice.

Eight

The day came and brought no dwindling of enthusiasm. Since the prime necessity was peace and quiet, punctuated by regular stimulants for the brain, I asked Sebastian to glue himself to the telephone, to inform all callers except Robin and my agent that I was in the South of France, and to bring fresh supplies of black coffee every hour on the hour.

He did not accept these instructions in quite the servile manner I could have wished.

'What about the shopping then? Who's to do that?'

'What's the matter? Are we out of coffee?'

'Soon will be, at this rate. I was thinking of lunch.'

'Then stop thinking about it, and please do as I ask.'

'You wouldn't like me to slip round the corner and fetch a little something in?'

I preserved a majestic calm and told him that, if he stepped outside his order by so much as a centimetre, I would get Robin to lock him up for three months on charges to be decided later.

Having disposed of these weighty domestic affairs, I set about drawing up my case for the prosecution, versus Birdie Hawkes.

The inspiration of this identikit Mr B/Jasmine Hawkes character had followed from the concept of Robin's case overlapping the province of Julian's diary, and the more I examined it the more logical it appeared.

Having cast Jasmine in the role of blackmailer, which her sudden access of wealth made it easy to do, it was gratifying to find how neatly the other items fell into place.

Even I, in reading the first volume of the diary, had come upon enough material to keep me in luxury for years had I possessed a blackmailing turn of mind. How much more of this gilt-edged commodity, I argued, would have accrued to one whose adult memories stretched ten or fifteen years farther back than mine.

At this point, I became slightly perplexed by the fact that Jasmine had elected to cut herself off from the rich vein, when the source had barely been tapped. However, whatever the reason, it went far to substantiate her guilt. Despite my drowsy state of the previous night, I retained a distinct recollection of Robin's telling me that Mr B had vanished without a trace.

A graver stumbling block was Betty's part in all this and, whichever way I looked at it, her involvement was too obvious to be ignored. In a cowardly attempt to push the thought away, I picked up the *Times* and meticulously checked all the clues Toby had missed in the crossword. However, even this charming exercise proved inadequate for the purpose, and, in the faint hope of finding something to divert the puzzled mind, I turned to the front page.

The first thing that caught my eye was a photograph of Peter Hitchens, he to whom I had yielded my place beside the guest of honour at our party. In recent years he had become celebrated less for the quality of his performances than for the number of his divorces, plus a lamentable tendency to get fighting drunk in nightclubs, and, in the expectation of yet another fiasco on these lines, I idly skimmed the text. It stated, in bald terms, that he had been found dead from an overdose in his London flat. The police were investigating and foul play was not suspected.

I do not know why it shook me so badly. He had never been a favourite of mine and, lately, had become so unbalanced as to be practically outside the realms of normal communication. Nevertheless, he had once been handsome and talented, we had sometimes laughed together, and he had been in our house only forty-eight hours before his lonely squalid death.

Sensations of outrage and disbelief soon gave way to calmer feelings, but the incident was to haunt me for days, and one immediate effect was to cut my own problems down to size. I no longer baulked at acknowledging the fact that Betty's abrupt departure from our party had not been due to anything Robin had said, but purely to the fact that she had recognised him as Detective Inspector Price of the C.I.D.

Once faced, it lost much of its sting and numerous mitigating factors came flying to the rescue. First was the reminder that Betty's career had taken her into so many different worlds that there would have been nothing strange in Robin's having figured briefly in it, perhaps in some connection which had distressing associations for her. Then, too, her concern over the disappearance of Jasmine by no means indicated a guilty conscience. It was much more likely that, suspecting her of blackmail, but lacking proof, she had tried to keep track of her by whichever means came to hand.

I was so encouraged by this whitewashing exercise that I could not wait to smother the last remaining doubts and decided that the best method would be to coerce or trick Betty into laying some of her cards on the table. I therefore dialled Thurgoods' number and asked to speak to her.

Keeping ulterior motives out of it, I said: 'I have news for you. Is this the right moment?'

'Yes, but make it sharpish.'

I told her about Jasmine's letter, and she said: 'Well, that doesn't get us much further, does it?'

'The only thing is, it was signed "Birdie", which was his own special name for her. So, if it's a forgery, it must have been done by someone in the know.'

'Who said it was a forgery?'

'No one, but you've been acting so mysterious that I concluded you thought it might be.'

'Then you concluded wrong.'

'Of course, if it was a forgery,' I ploughed on, 'the most likely culprit would be the recipient; but that doesn't fit, because he's as cross as two sticks about it. Also, wouldn't it follow that he must have bumped her off? In which case, where would he have concealed the corpse?'

'For God's sake, shut up, Tessa. There's no telling where these extensions extend to. You'll get us both in trouble, if you don't look out.'

'Well, how about meeting for lunch? Somewhere where we can talk in private.'

'I can't see that there's anything to talk about.'

'Well, you've really got me worrying about all this. I've had a few ideas, which I'd like to discuss with you.'

Doubtless preferring that such ideas, after the sample I had given her, should be poured into her ears before anyone else's, she consented to this. We agreed on a restaurant near Piccadilly and I should really have been content to leave it at that. Unfortunately, there is a certain morbid satisfaction in passing on bad news, and, before she could ring off, I said: 'Oh, by the way, you remember Peter Hitchens?'

'I think so. Didn't I meet him with you? Why?'

I told her, and she seemed as stunned as I had been,

for half a minute passed before she answered. But a shock of that kind takes people in different ways and when she spoke again her voice was harsh and indifferent:

'That's too bad. Well, I must go now, Tessa. Goodbye.'

Sebastian arrived with the eleven o'clock coffee ration, a few minutes after I put the receiver down.

'Cousin Toby is up and about, with his hat on,' he announced. 'Don't blame me; I never went near him.'

'He's leaving us, is he? Well, I intend to be up and about with my hat on, in a couple of ticks. There'll be no lunch, and we're out to dinner, too. We're going to a first night.'

'Lucky old you! Mind if I take a toddle in that case? I feel quite gasping for breath, shut up indoors all day.'

'Toddle away,' I told him. 'Just so long as you're back by twelve-thirty.'

Some trick of memory had brought my Indian brooch to mind, and when he had gone I formed myself into a search-party for the second-best jewellery. I found it eventually in the pockets of a satchel-like container, which some misguided manufacturer had put on the market as a receptacle for women's stockings. I scooped it all out, and was pleased to see one or two pieces I had forgotten I possessed, but the brooch was not among them. I made a mental note to ask Sandy to start negotiations with the insurance company, or, better still, to have one of her brainwaves and tell me where I had put it.

(ii)

'Not that he was back by twelve-thirty,' I told Robin,

when we were dressing for what Sebastian called the Preemeer, 'but I don't suppose it mattered. People don't normally ring up with important offers at lunch-time.'

'I might have rung up with an important offer.'

'Not for Sebastian, though, so it wouldn't have done you any good, if he had been here.'

'The point is that he might have been able to tell me where you were.'

'I was window-shopping in the Burlington Arcade. My lunch date fell through.'

'I see. Well, how much longer are you going to be? We shall be frightfully late, if you don't get a move on.'

There was a rare note of irritability in his voice, which boded something graver than the perennial grievance of Sebastian's shortcomings, or even the worse persecution of having to struggle with a black tie, and I said: 'Has something happened to annoy you?'

'You could put it like that. Mr B is back in my life.'

'Oh no? Another of those postcards?'

'That's right.'

'And Madam X is creating merry hell, I take it?'

'Oh, we have a different X now. This is victim No. Two.'

'Oh, my goodness! Although, in a way, you should be pleased, Robin. It gives you a whole new field; and you said, yourself, that it was inaction that you most hated.'

'We won't get much action out of this one.'

'You mean that this X is as cagey as the other?'

'Much, much cagier; and no chance of ever loosening up.'

I digested this in silence, while some nasty little threads of conjecture knotted themselves together, behind the face of the fretful sheepdog which confronted me in the glass.

'Any common denominator between the first and second X?' I forced myself at last to ask.

'Just one.'

'Oh!'

'Unfortunately, it's one which I could well do without. It may be pure coincidence; I hope so, but it will have to be followed up. You must be ready by now, surely?'

'As ready as I'll ever be,' I admitted.

'Who stood you up?' he asked, as we slid across London in our hired limousine, 'I forgot to ask.'

'Only Betty Haverstock. We were supposed to meet, but she couldn't make it.'

'Ah! Pressure of work, no doubt?'

'That's right. There was a message, when I arrived, saying she was tied up. It wasn't important.'

'Just a little puzzling, perhaps?'

The car had halted at the approach to Whitehall, wedged in between two buses. There was an *Evening News* stall on the pavement, a few feet away. On one of the placards were scrawled the words: STAR'S DEATH: LATEST, and I stared at them with a sinking heart, until the car inched forward again and carried them out of sight.

'Just a little,' I agreed.

Nine

One of the few snags I had encountered in married life was the obligation to account to one other person for one's behaviour; and this was never more acute than in cases where the behaviour was unlikely to obtain the other person's blessing and approval. The conspiracy over Julian's diary fell sharply into this category and, although the shock of Peter's death and anxiety about Betty had contributed something to the postponement of a full confession to Robin, I knew that they could not excuse it indefinitely and had resolved to acquaint him of the arrangement, just as soon as the right moment arrived.

So it was with equal degrees of relief and disappointment that I awoke on Wednesday to find he had already left for the office. His message added that he would be home about the usual time. This was an elastic phrase, but did not normally encompass anything earlier than seven. Since I had invited Julian for six o'clock, the right moment was clearly still some way off.

The dilemma of Sebastian was exactly opposite, for I regarded it as essential that no hint of the diary's whereabouts should ever reach those inquisitive ears. Since unsolicited permission to take a toddle at six in the evening, would arouse such a passion of curiosity as no evasions of mine could assuage, I saw that the only solution was to enlist outside aid.

I therefore sent him out to buy all the papers, so that

I could see how many of them had featured our arrival at the Preemeer, and, as soon as he had scuttled away on this errand, I telephoned my agent.

I requested her to call back in an hour's time, with the news that important documents would be ready for my signature by six o'clock, and that I should send a messenger to collect them. He, of course, would be Sebastian, and she was to keep him waiting for at least half an hour on any pretext she cared to dream up.

Meanwhile, some familiar lumbering noises from next door signified that Sandy was at her post, and she came bursting into my room, just as I replaced the receiver. In addition to the mail, she carried a tray, with teapot and matching accoutrements.

'Good morrow to you! The henchman appears to have skedaddled, and I thought you might care for a cuppa.'

'Brilliant wheeze!' I replied, slipping into the vernacular.

In fact, I did not much care for Sandy's treacly brew, but the merry tinkle of teacups struck exactly the right note for our forthcoming chat.

'How are you?' I inquired. 'And how's Bobs?'

'Not so dusty.'

'Oh good! And I hope that means you won't have to dash straight home this evening. Someone I want you to meet is coming here at six, and it just might lead to an interesting Monday job, if you're not already fixed up.'

'What ho! More relatives in a stew about their income tax?'

'No, this is a director of Thurgoods that I've known for ages. He's a trifle batty, but loaded with lolly, so you could sting him for as much as you liked.'

'Come now, old girl, you know me better than that!'

'Yes, I do, but this job would only be for a month or two, so you'd be entirely justified in bumping up your normal rates.'

'What sort of work is it?'

I had guessed that its temporary nature would appeal to her, and more particularly to Bobs, and her question showed that I was on the right lines.

'Mostly typing,' I said airily. 'Nothing very strenuous.'

'Oh, just a sec, old top. I don't know if that kind of routine work could be quite up my street. I prefer something I can get the old teeth into.'

'You could get them into this all right. Listen, and I'll give you the gen.'

She did so with keen attention, while I described the set-up on Thurgoods's second floor, harping on the secret and confidential nature of the diaries, and she said thoughtfully: 'I see. A bit hush-hush, what?'

'Which is exactly why I thought of you.'

'Thanks,' she said, blinking rapidly. 'Thanks muchly. Jolly nice to know one's appreciated and you're a brick to have thought of me. Mind if I chew it over with Bobs, before I give a yea or nay?'

'That's the whole idea. I wanted to give you the outline and now it's up to you.'

'Fair enough,' Sandy agreed, and we moved on to the subject of the lost brooch, and other matters requiring her expert attention.

Nor did my agent fail me, for her call came through on the appointed dot. I was fairly certain that Sebastian would have listened in on a downstairs extension, but I relayed the message with a solemn face, and prodded him again about it after tea.

'Off in a mo,' he replied. 'Better take a ticker, hadn't I?'

'You'll have time to get there by bus, I'd have thought. The papers won't be ready till six-thirty.'

'Six o'clock, you said.'

'Oh yes, so I did. Give him a pound out of the petty cash, will you, Sandy?'

'Ta ever so,' Sebastian said, grabbing the note.

'That young scamp imposes on you,' Sandy said, when he had gone. 'I could tell from the look in his eye that he meant to pocket the money and travel by bus.'

'Oh, do you think so?' I asked in shocked terms, the same thought having occurred to me, although, unfortunately, we were both wrong.

'And what a juggins you are! I could have fetched those papers for you, in the Mini.'

'No, your time is much too valuable. Besides, you must be here when our gentleman arrives. Come down when you're ready.'

'Righty-ho,' she agreed, swivelling round to the typewriter, and I went downstairs to set the stage for the next act.

Our drawing-room, like so many of its period, contained and alcove on each side of the fireplace. The one on the left was fitted with shelves from floor to ceiling, but its opposite number had been divided in half, with shelves at the top and a cupboard below. We had never used this cupboard, because it had so far been beyond our powers to decide whether to do away with it, or have a matching one on the other side. Either would have achieved the symmetry so dear to both our hearts, but only time could show which would be more practical. There was a key to this cupboard, which I had hidden in a snuff box, from where I now retrieved it.

I glanced round the room, noting the prim little

flower arrangements which Sandy's large and capable hands had fashioned, and at everything wearing its neat Wednesday look; and I saw that all that remained was for the curtain to rise:

'Overture and Beginners, Please!' I said to myself, going to the kitchen for ice.

(ii)

I had once endeavoured to explain to Robin, who, for a brief period, had been in favour of my giving up my career, that the material rewards were among the least of its attractions. The fact was that the discipline and clockwork precision, which the profession demanded, provided a perfect antidote to the haphazardness of real life.

Luckily, Robin had soon come round to my point of view, having the grace to admit that our lives were slightly less chaotic when I was working than when all my energies could be devoted to sorting out other people's lives for them; but, had it still been needed, the events of that Wednesday evening would have provided the supreme example of the point I had tried to illustrate. If Julian had been taking part in a play, he could have been counted on to bounce in, dead on cue, since failure to do so would have met with icy looks and possible loss of employment. The mere fact of being a private individual enabled him to blunder through life, missing his entrances and ruining the performance for everyone else, with total impunity.

Sandy and I were obliged to *ad lib* our way through the whole of the first forty minutes, by which time we had scraped the bottom of the barrel, so far as the iniquities of the Ealing shopkeepers and the sly practices of Mrs Goldsmith were concerned. As I rose to refill her glass, she said awkwardly: 'No desire to leave you in the lurch, old thing, but I ought to be crashing along.'

I had no valid excuse to detain her, and yet I was reluctant to see my scheme fall to pieces. I had built it up so painstakingly that I was quite in love with it and the end was becoming subservient to the means. So I proposed a stalling move, whereby Sandy should telephone Bobs and find out how the land lay. She pounced on this offer and I could hear the old brute growling away at the other end, but explanations were barely under way when the doorbell rang.

I darted into the hall, but the front door was already open and in marched Julian, with Sebastian hard on his heels.

'Ooh, just in time,' he panted. 'Sorry I'm late, madam, but they kept me ever so long at the office. Ask them, if you don't believe me. Ooh, allow me to take that for you, sir,' he added, making a dive at Julian's suitcase.

'Kindly leave it alone,' Julian snarled, clutching the case with both hands and glaring about him. Clearly, he was in a black mood, and the attempt to deprive him of his precious burden had torn a few more shreds in his frayed nerves. It was equally apparent that Sebastian was deeply offended by the snub, and I said quickly: 'You've got the package? Be an angel and put it in my room. We shan't need you for half an hour.'

'What about the ice and that?'

'I've seen to it, so please do as I ask.'

He gave me one of his sly looks and walked towards the stairs.

'Sorry about all that,' I said to Julian, 'but it's your fault, for being so late.'

'If you knew what hell I've been through, you wouldn't nag,' he said tearfully.

'What happened?'

'Can't you guess? My sister-in-law smelt a rat. She must have seen Barnes bring the empty case in and guessed what was up. She came upstairs just before closing time and planted herself outside my office, waiting to see what I'd do.'

'And what did you do?'

'I was trapped. We always keep the bar going till seven and she had a perfect right to sit there, if she chose. In the end, Barnes had to bribe a taxi to wait at the main entrance, and then get her attention while I slipped out to the lift.'

'Did she catch you?'

'No, Barnes was magnificent, but it was a damn close thing. She dived after me and I only just slammed the doors in time. It was the most humiliating situation you can imagine. A man of my position, sneaking off his own premises, like some petty thief! And, for all I know, she may have followed me and made a note of this address. I'll kill that woman one of these days, I know I will.'

'Calm down and come and have a drink.'

'All right. God, isn't everything bloody, though? And now I suppose you're going to tell me that this secretary person has left? Just my wretched luck!'

I opened the drawing-room door and found that, despite the interval, Sandy was still on the telephone. She glanced up as we entered and it was evident from her flushed face and strained look, that she had been getting the brow-beating of a lifetime. Nevertheless, I was unprepared for what happened next.

I had my back to the room and was pouring Julian a drink, when I heard the receiver being replaced, and turned to see Sandy, with a handkerchief to her face, moving jerkily, but with rapid steps to the door. Thrusting the glass into Julian's hand I caught her up in the hall. She was clutching the banister knob with one hand and mopping her face with the other.

'Sorry about that, old dear,' she said, in a pathetic travesty of the hearty manner. 'Don't often turn on the waterworks, but one does get a bit browned off sometimes, doesn't one?'

I agreed that one did, adding: 'But is anything seriously wrong, or is it just ... ?'

'Or is it just the aged P playing up a bit? Frankly, your guess is as good as mine, but I'll have to scarper. You do understand?'

I understood only too well. It was the first time that Sandy's facade had cracked, or that she had dropped so much as a hint that all was not lovely in the Garden of Ealing, and I judged her to be near breaking-point to have betrayed so much.

'Yes, of course. Off you go, this very minute. Give me a buzz later on, though, and let me know the score. I shall worry like mad until I hear from you.'

'I'll do that, never ye fear; and thanks for being so ripping about it.'

'Don't drive too fast, and I'll see you next week,' I replied in my rippingest voice.

'Just have to keep our fingers crossed, old lady.'

This was far from the reassurance the old lady had been seeking, and I returned to the drawing-room, weighed down by misgivings.

I had long suspected that there was a dash of the manic depressive in Julian, and that he needed only the tiniest shove to send him spinning into one abyss or the other. Even so, I was faintly astounded by the transformation which had occurred. Whether it was due to the sight of someone else in worse straits than himself, or to the outsize whisky, was impossible to say, but he was frisking about the room like a silly puppy.

'What a charming place!' he said, twirling his empty glass. 'You've got quite good taste.'

'The compliment would sound even better without that note of surprise.'

'Oh, I was just teasing. Where's your sense of humour?'

'I'm a bit worried about Sandy, if you must know.'

'You mean that hysterical female? Yes, what a performance! She's one of those repressed spinsters; I recognise the type at a glance. What did you say her name was?'

'Phelps Sanderson. No one can ever remember it, so we call her Sandy.'

I had rejected the impulse to fly to her defence. It would have been sheer waste of effort, with Julian in this excitable mood; and, since the chances of a Monday job with him now seemed distinctly remote, my one object was to conclude my business with him and send him on his way.

I indicated the alcove cupboard and requested him to deposit the case inside without more ado. Needless to say, more ado was instantly forthcoming and he raised a score of objections, including the unforeseen one that the heat from the fire would warp the case and frizzle its contents.

'We don't have fires in May,' I snapped, sacrificing truth to expediency.

'But right here in your living-room, Tessa! It seems so public somehow.'

'That is the charm of it,' I said. 'Like Edgar Allan Poe's letter, if you see what I mean?'

Perhaps he didn't, his reading having been confined

mainly to his own works, but he must have seen that my heels were dug in, for, with only a few more grumbles, he pushed the heavy case inside. Panting with relief I locked the door and handed him the key.

'I shall want it back as soon as you've made other arrangements, and you can't make them too fast for me.'

'Is this the only key?'

'It is.'

'But supposing Lavender got hold of it? You can take it from me, she's more than capable of stealing it.'

'It wouldn't do her much good, would it? Unless, of course, you mean to put a label on it, with the address on one side and a plan of the house on the other?'

He was wearing his mulish look again and I was bracing myself for another round of opposition, when there was a fresh development, equally trying to the nerves in its way. The door opened and in walked Robin.

'Oh, hallo, darling!' I gushed. 'Julian was just leaving, so how lovely that you're in time to meet him! This is my husband, Julian; and you must be careful what you say, because it will all be written down and used in evidence.'

Robin frowned at me thoughtfully, as though searching for a clue to this taradiddle, which in fact was simply a means of giving Julian time to collect himself. He was blushing and twittering, like the lover in a bedroom farce, but at least he had the presence of mind to slip the key in his pocket.

'Tessa is rather apt to get carried away,' Robin said kindly. 'Was it always so?'

'Oh yes, rather!' Julian tittered obsequiously. 'That is, she's got a terrific sense of humour, so I never mind what she says.'

Robin took this in his stride, saying calmly: 'Have you time for another drink, before you go?'

'No, no, thanks most awfully. Just dropped by to say Hallo. Must dash now. Well, Tessa, it's been tremendous fun,' he said, dithering towards the door.

Following him into the hall, I said: 'Sorry my great idea fizzled out, but I'll try and think up something else.'

'Oh, I thought we managed it all splendidly.'

'I meant my plan for finding you a secretary.'

'Oh that? Only a temporary set-back, I feel sure. I expect she'll be most competent. I'll be in touch with you about it.'

The mood had turned euphoric again, and he gambolled off down the steps, waving his arms in a demented attempt to hail a passing taxi, which already contained a full load of passengers.

I remained propped against the front door for a few seconds, inhaling deep, reviving gusts of air. Sebastian, coming downstairs in a clean white suit and a smug look to match, caught me in the act.

'Coast clear now?' he asked, following me into the drawing-room.

Robin had retreated behind the evening paper. 'Sorry about my dotty friend,' I said, thinking that the evening was certainly providing me with a variety of people to apologise to.

'I am afraid I scared him off,' he said, not sounding very regretful about it.

Sebastian, who had been busying himself with the empty glasses, in an irritatingly virtuous manner, spoke up: 'I see the gentleman went off without his suitcase. Want me to take it round to him after dinner?'

'No, he didn't,' I said, without due reflection.

'He did, you know. I happened to be glancing out

of my window and I saw him on the pavement. He was waving his hands in the air and I thought to myself: "Ha ha! So, after all that, you've gone and forgotten it!"'

'After all what?' Robin inquired with mild interest.

'All nothing,' I said firmly. 'Julian brought some documents here, which he wants typed in a hurry and Sandy has agreed to do it. She's taken the case home with her.'

I had my back to the cupboard and, to frustrate any extra-sensory perceptions, which might be hovering, concentrated fiercely on my fictitious picture of Sandy speeding westwards in the Mini, the suitcase reposing innocently on the back seat.

Perhaps they both suspected me of something less than frankness, but I had gambled on Sandy's sudden departure having caught Sebastian while he was temporarily absent from his spy-post and on Robin's indifference to see me through.

One should never underestimate masculine intuition, however, for we were no sooner alone than he said:

'Are we dining in tonight?'

'Yes, we are.'

'No one coming?'

'No. Why do you ask?'

'We've had such a rackety time lately. I thought it might be fun to have dinner served in here, on that trolley thing.'

'Great! Why don't we?'

'We could light the fire and put our feet up, and ... Oh, my dear Tessa, what are you gaping at me like that for?'

The right moment had come at last, but, with Sebastian flitting in and out, I had to let it go by. Unfortunately, Robin's relaxed and expansive mood grew more pronounced as the evening wore on, and it would have been sheer vandalism to destroy it by introducing disagreeable topics. So nothing was said that evening about the hidden suitcase.

Ten

There had been no word from Sandy during our cosy fireside evening, nor by the time I went out on Thursday, for an afternoon session at the photographer's. On my way home, I called on my agent to return an envelope containing blank contract forms which she had lent for props.

'Everything go according to plan?' she asked.

'No, but that wasn't your fault. I should have asked you to keep the messenger here until midnight.'

'I'm thankful you didn't, my darling. I wouldn't want that creep, Sebastian, on the premises for long. Him and his compulsive snooping.'

'Well, rather inquisitive, I admit, but only over trifles. He likes to be *au courant*.'

'That's putting it mildly.'

I was still churning over this remark when I arrived back at Beacon Square at six o'clock. Undeniably, there was a consensus of opinion among the initiates that Sebastian was getting above himself, and I braced myself to deliver a stern lecture on the subject.

It was a waste of brace, however, because he was not at home. Just before my blood came to the boil, I perceived a note on the hall table, which instantly brought the temperature down. It read as follows: 'Phone's on the blink. Have slipped out to call-box to report. Your lady-friend is holding the fort. S.'

I had not been expecting callers and I sped through to the drawing-room to see which lady-friend the wheel of fortune had sent us in our hour of need. There was no one there, but one notable addition to the furnishings. This was a large, shop-wrapped parcel propped up on the sofa.

There is nothing to compare with an unexpected present, for blunting life's little pinpricks, and I fell upon it with eager hands. A moment later, I fell smartly back again, for a close-up view of the label had shown it to be one of Thurgoods', and the sight of it, within two feet of the alcove cupboard, had unnerved me completely.

Sebastian returned as I was wrestling with yards of Sellotape which would have been more suitably employed in holding the parts of an aeroplane together, and I sent him to the kitchen for assorted weapons.

'Ooh, ooh, whatever can it be?' he asked, hopping about, in a frenzy of excitement, as I plunged my hands into a sea of shavings and tissue paper.

'It is a Regency book carrier,' I replied, dragging it forth.

'There, now! Oh well, some people have all the luck, don't they?'

'Don't they just?' I said, ramming it back in the box.

'What's up, then? Isn't it what you ordered?'

'No.'

'Pity! They must have brought it to the wrong address.'

'Hardly,' I replied. 'Since my name is on the label, and Lady Haverstock does not normally make mistakes of that magnitude.'

'Oh, it's from her, is it?'

'Isn't it?' I asked slowly. 'You mean it wasn't she who brought it?'

'Well, not in person no. It was this other one. I

didn't catch her name, but she asked for you and said she was a friend.'

I sank on to the sofa and closed my eyes:

'Describe this person, Sebastian. The full word picture.'

He was first-rate at that kind of thing, being acutely observant, and two or three graphic phrases confirmed my worst fears.

'Now, let's get this straight,' I said. 'This female came to the door and asked for me, and you said I was out. Right?'

'Right.'

'Then what?'

'She asked when you'd be back, and I said it might be any time. Five minutes, or then again, a couple of hours. No telling, I said.'

'But you invited her in?'

'Oh, I never. She was in already, by that time. She said she'd brought this parcel for you, but there was something she wanted to explain, so could she wait?'

'So you showed her in here and then did your slipping out bit? How long were you away?'

'You've left something out. First of all, she said she was sorry to call unexpectedly, but did we know our phone was out of order?'

'And did we?'

'Of course not. It hadn't rung all afternoon, but that's nothing special, is it? Still, I did remember you saying this morning that you'd been waiting for a call from Miss Sanderson, and that hadn't come through either, so I said to myself: "Well, maybe it's on the level."'

'So saying, you left her alone in here and nipped out to the call-box?'

'No, I wouldn't be so daft. People often make the

excuse they've tried to phone and couldn't get through. You keep leaving out great chunks of the script. What I did was, I asked her if she'd fancy a cup of tea because I'd got the kettle on, and she said she was dying for one, so I went to make it; but the first thing I did was try the kitchen extension.'

'And you mean to tell me that it really was out of order?'

'Yes, of course,' he said innocently. 'Why else would I have gone out? Specially when it was true about how you might be in at any minute,' he added as an afterthought.

'So?'

'I brought her tea in here, and said would she mind if I slipped out for a tick, to report our number being on the blink, the phone being our life's blood, so to speak.'

'And she didn't mind at all?'

'No, she was ever so nice about it. Why the third degree? She hasn't pinched anything, has she?'

I had been prepared for something on these lines and replied gravely: 'I can't be certain, but from your description I'm pretty sure she's a well-known thief. Scotland Yard have known about her for months.'

'Oh cripes! Do you really think so? Ooh, aren't people wicked? She seemed ever such a nice person, too. What are you going to do? Ring the Inspector and tell him about it?'

'You seem to have forgotten that our line is out of order.'

'Oh, they're quick workers, when they want to be. It might be on by now.'

'I shouldn't be at all surprised. Let's try.'

He unhooked the receiver and handed it to me. It was as dead as a stage dummy.

'There now!' Sebastian said, clicking his tongue. 'Oh, it's just like a thriller, isn't it? You and me alone here, cut off from the outside world! Want me to run out and phone the Inspector?'

'No, what we need first is careful thought. You had better start by bringing me a strong drink and some wet towels for my head.'

As soon as he had gone, I bounded off the sofa and knelt down in front of the alcove cupboard. If there had been a magnifying-glass handy, I should doubtless have waved it over some hairline scratches round the keyhole, but nothing more would have been learnt than that the door was still locked and might or might not have been opened, during Mrs Teddy's solitary vigil.

The rattle of glasses sent me scurrying back to the sofa. Sebastian set the tray down and remained standing in front of me, looking furtive and tearful.

'Out with it,' I said.

'It's not my fault, I swear, but you're going to be hopping mad.'

'I'll be the judge of that.'

'Well, I slipped up to your bedroom, see? Thought I'd take a dekko. You know, all your jewellery and that.'

'And what did you find?'

'Well, nothing; except, you know, your receiver was off. So that's what must have done it. I'm ever so sorry, but it wasn't me, honestly.'

The trouble with Sebastian was that I could never be a hundred per cent certain that he was lying. Furthermore, before I could decide whether his doing so made the present situation more or less complicated, the telephone rang.

Swooping on it with a shriek of joy, he handed me

the receiver in the triumphant manner of one for whom all troubles were over. But, as it turned out, they were only just beginning.

(ii)

'Oh, hallo!' I said. 'How are you, and how's Bobs?'

'Flourishing, thanks. Flap's over. Just as well I bashed off, though. Mrs G had been on the warpath again and the fat would have been well and truly in the fire.'

'My goodness, yes! I can't wait to hear about it. On Wednesday.'

There was silence and my heart began the descent to my boots. When it had reached knee level, she said:

'Look here, old scout, could I pop round for a chat, some time tomorrow?'

'Tomorrow being Friday?'

'As ever was. Would one-thirty suit? I'm generally through with my Friday job by one, and I could get a snack on my way.'

'No, you must have lunch here. I insist.'

'Awfully good of you, old duck.'

'It's not bad news?'

'No, but I feel I behaved like an awful clot, in front of your Mr Brown yesterday. It was a bit rotten letting you down, too, after all your trouble. Bobs and I had a good old natter about it and, well, if you think there might still be a chance, I'd be glad to take the job on.'

'Oh, you bet there would be.'

'Jolly dee. All the same, I'd feel a bit of a Charlie, ringing him up, myself. Bobs said you'd know better than me how to do it tactfully, and I thought, if I were to tank round tomorrow, we might chew the rag a bit?'

I told her that I had to call at Thurgoods in the morning and would sound Julian out.

The conversation had just closed when Robin arrived and, naturally, became quite a bundle of curiosity about the large, dishevelled parcel, which still occupied most of the sofa.

I dug the book carrier out again and he was more enthusiastic than I had bargained for, claiming that it was just what he wanted for his bedside table.

'Then want must be your master, for it is going back tomorrow.'

'Why? Isn't it the one you bought?'

'Yes, but as you know Thurgoods bought it back again. What's more, I've already had one free drink under false pretences.'

'Then why have they sent it?'

'I'm Yours Sincerely, Baffled. Some ploy of Betty's, perhaps.'

I did not refer to some of the other possibilities, for it no longer seemed worth confessing about the suitcase in the cupboard, with the chances now equal that it was no longer there.

'And no note in this envelope?' Robin asked.

'Oh, is that an envelope? I thought it was just the label, not stuck on properly.'

He was right, of course, and there was a letter inside, signed L. Brown (Director), which read as follows:

Madam,

It has come to our notice that the enclosed Georgian Mahogany Book Carrier was purchased by your good self, as the result of an error by one of our staff. Since this transaction was entered into by you in good faith, we are returning the article herewith and trust you will accept our apologies for any inconvenience you may have suffered. Yours faithfully ...

'Very pompous,' I said, passing the note to Robin. I was thinking that it could be genuine, too. I had only Julian's word for it that she was such a villain, and he was notoriously unreliable.

'So that's settled, then,' Robin said. 'We keep it.'

I felt too confused to argue, and ready to believe that any action I might take would be the wrong one. So I agreed to let sleeping dogs lie, though privately convinced that at least one of them would soon be aroused, and yapping down the telephone that the key to our cupboard was missing.

However, nothing of the kind occurred and, as the evening wore on, I was lulled into the belief that Mrs Teddy's visit had been as guileless as she made out.

Eleven

Before setting out on Friday morning I made Sebastian accompany me on a tour of the house to ensure that every telephone was in its correct position, and also gave him permission to slip out for a couple of hours at lunch-time. He and Sandy did not hit it off particularly well and I thought her style might be cramped by his tripping around and pulling faces during our chat.

It was a warm, mellow day and, having been inspired to wear my new pink trouser suit and cowboy hat, I loped through Green Park and all the way to Piccadilly Circus, pretending it was the big scene from *High Noon*. A lope of that distance takes its toll, however and, on reaching Thurgoods, I collapsed into a Jacobean chair, which was parked beside Betty's desk. I had already seen that she was dealing with a customer, a mean-faced, toad-like creature, who could have been sold off, himself, to any collector of gargoyles. Evidently he was a rich old monster, though, because Betty was giving him the full treatment, and I reckoned I had about ten minutes in hand for a refreshing snooze.

Ten seconds after closing my eyes, I was startled into life by shrill, staccato yaps, followed by a piercing nip on the ankle, and saw a vicious-looking, undershot hearthrug, crouched snarling at my feet. It had been tethered by its lead to a table leg, but the sight of two defenceless ankles must have brought out the blood lust, for it had slipped its collar which lay on the floor still attached to the trailing lead.

Alerted by the rumpus, Betty and her client bustled over. The toadlike creature gathered up his brutish pet, which he admonished in notably affectionate terms, and Betty glared at me in fury: 'For God's sake, Tessa, did you have to?'

'It wasn't my fault. The little beast set on me. It's lucky for you I've had my tetanus shots.'

'You're not really hurt, are you?'

'I most certainly am,' I replied, raising my trouser leg, to reveal the fang marks.

'Well, I'm dreadfully sorry, Tessa, but you do choose the worst possible moments to create your dramas. There's a first-aid box in my desk, Put something on it and I'll be with you in a moment.'

The toad had remained aloof from this muttered exchange, cuddling his nasty animal and blinking his hooded eyes in a vaguely malevolent fashion. When Betty had finished with me, he stalked ahead of her, back to the piece of furniture they had been haggling over before the interruption.

She returned a few minutes later, as I was applying the bandaid.

'Did you make a killing?' I asked her.

'Not yet, but I have hopes. He wants the marquetry desk put aside until he's talked to his wife.'

'Isn't that what they all say?'

'A good many do, but I've a feeling this one means business. For one thing, he's already paid for a famille rose bowl; cash, too, so he'll be back all right.'

'Twenty-five pounds worth?'

'A lot more than that, my dear,' she answered, brandishing a wad of notes. 'Why?'

'Just wondered if it rated a drink in the Boardroom.'

'Yes, I told him about that, but he said he'd rather wait until he'd decided about the desk, and then he might have a couple, ho ho. And now, if you've finished coddling yourself, perhaps you'll move over and let me make out my receipt. What are you here for, anyway?'

Evidently, she was still inclined to blame me for the fact that her deal had not been clinched, and I said warily, 'I had a visitor yesterday; a Greek bearing gifts. I wondered if you could throw any light on it.'

'No. Why should I?'

'Only that it was your Mrs Ted, bearing the book carrier you once sold me, in an idle moment. Does that convey anything?'

'No. So far as I was aware, it had gone back to its rightful owner and that was that.'

'Well, it wasn't that, because now it's come back to its wrongful owner again.'

'Well, I warned you she was a crackpot,' Betty said indifferently, 'And, if that's all you've come for, you'd better buzz off and let me get on with some work. Friday is my busy day.'

'It's a busy one for me, too, I'm on my way to see Mr Arthur Julian.'

'Again? You two are very thick, aren't you?'

'Yes, aren't we? He's thicker than I am, actually; and, anyway, it's mostly your doing, you and your Jasmine.'

'You haven't found out anything useful, I suppose?'

'No, but I'm still at it. Something may turn up.'

'Well, as I've said before, watch your step.'

This warning reminded me of my injured ankle, and I examined it for signs of swelling or septicaemia before trying my weight on it. Fortunately, I felt no pain at all, though did not let on to Betty, lest the postponement of the marquetry sale still rankled. With a gallant wave of the hand, I hobbled to the lift.

(ii)

I had not intended to refer to Lavender's visit, unless Julian first admitted having lost the key, but in fact, I could not have done so, for the only people in evidence on the second floor were Barnes and my old friends, Peregrine and Joannie, seated side by side at the bar. The mechanical nod with which Joannie had greeted my entrance, hardened to solid wood when Peregrine rolled off his stool and wrapped me in a warm embrace.

'Entrancing!' he said loudly, stumbling back a pace or two, for a mid-shot view, and knocking his stool over in the process. 'Quite utterly entrancing, and just the soupçonest crazy. Wouldn't you agree, Joannie?'

'Stop staring at the poor girl,' Joannie said irritably. 'You'll embarrass her.'

'Oh, be your age, Joannie. Why do you suppose she's got up like this, if not to be stared at? Isn't that right, my love?'

'It is something I never think about, one way or the other,' I said. 'I might get the wrong impression of myself.'

'Oh, bravo!' Peregrine said, laughing extravagantly at this fatuous observation.

'Good morning, madam, and what may I have the pleasure?' Barnes inquired, putting an end to the first round.

'A glass of your dry one, please. Is Mr Julian around?'

'Should be back at any minute, madam.'

'He'd better be,' Peregrine growled, turning truculent. 'Or we'll miss the first race.'

'Oh, you're going to the races?'

'That is usually the way to see the first race,' Joannie observed.

'And the redoubtable Barnes has been furnishing us with some red-hot tips.'

'Is it a big race today?' I asked the redoubtable Barnes.

'The Oaks, madam.'

'And what better, I asked myself, than for Joannie and me to drop in on old Julian and invite him to accompany us thither in his fast motor car?'

'Yes, but he's obviously not coming back, Perry.'

'That may be, but having put my hand to this plough, I do not lightly lerinquish it. With your permission, my dear girl, we shall give him another five minutes. Another of your excellent potions, please, Barnes!'

'Only an hour before the first race, sir.'

'They must run it without us. I am prepared to make that sacrifice for my old friend.'

'Who's going to win?' I asked Barnes.

'I rather fancy Fairy Gold, myself, madam; though Tara is favourite. Four to one, last I heard.'

'But, of course, you won't be there to see it?'

'As you know, that doesn't appeal to me. Besides, I have to be in attendance here at four o'clock.'

'You don't serve drinks all through the shopping hours?'

'No, madam. Just from ten till one-thirty, or thereabouts; and then again for an hour or two in the late afternoon.'

'It's a big gap. Can you get home?'

'I usually pop round to the local. They serve a decent hot dinner, and there's the telly, too.'

'So anyone could nip up here and help himself, while you're out?'

I had launched into this cross-examination less from curiosity than to cover a rather dangerous situation which seemed to be boiling up between my two companions. Joannie had relapsed into sullen silence and Peregrine, having knocked back his last drink with the speed of light, was glaring about him in a manner which indicated that he would shortly explode unless he found someone to pick a quarrel with. Barnes may have been alive to the danger, too, for he replied to my questions with as much earnest concentration as if I had had a perfect right to ask them. My last one had gone a little too far, however, for he said sternly: 'Oh no, madam. We do not have that class of customer here.'

I was rather fascinated by this pronouncement, wondering in what manner a customer would betray himself as belonging to that class; but Peregrine, provided at last with a target for his anger, knocked a dent in this interesting fantasy.

'Don't be fooled, my dear. This little old business is not run on such gentlemanly lines as Barnes would have you believe. He has omitted to mention that the whole floor is sealed off to outsiders during his visits to the local hostelry. There is a locking device on the lift door, for which only the nobs have keys. Am I not correct?'

'You should know, sir,' Barnes remarked cryptically, though perhaps not too cryptically for Peregrine, whose face became a shade more suffused, as he rapped the counter with his empty glass.

'The same again, please, Barnes, while we're about it. Make it a small one, this time.'

'We shall be here all night, at this rate,' Joannie said gloomily. 'Might as well give me another, too, Barnes.'

'Not for me, though,' I said, standing up. 'I've got a date, and I'm on my way.'

The top of the ascending lift came into view, and I felt sure that this heralded the return of Julian. Since his arrival at this point could be nothing but a hindrance, I stepped to one side and stood against the wall, meaning to dart into the lift as he emerged.

The door opened, but, instead of Julian, out tottered the Toad, followed by Betty, who sailed triumphantly forth, clutching a sheaf of documents. She caught sight of me, and, at the risk of dropping her precious papers, stuck both thumbs in the air and gave me a broad wink.

I descended to street level, abusing the fate which had timed my departure so clumsily. It would have been worth another few minutes to witness the encounter between those five ill-assorted people I had left behind on the second floor.

(iii)

It was as well, however, that I had resolved to come fairly carefully upon my hour, for I had to walk for miles before I found a taxi, and, even by sitting well forward and clenching my teeth, did not reach Beacon Square until twenty minutes to two.

Sandy's red Mini was parked outside and I stuck my head round the drawing-room door, to say that I would be with her in a couple of jiffs. The telephone started to ring as I came out of the bathroom, and I scooped it up and announced our number in a disguised voice, in case the caller were Julian. But there was no response, so I changed tactics and said 'Hallo' and 'Who's there?' about a dozen times, always with the strangest conviction that there really was someone listening silently to every word. It was no illusion, either, because just before my patience ran out there was a click and the dialling tone buzzed in my ear.

'Sorry to keep you waiting,' I said, as Sandy and I seated ourselves in the dining-room. 'It's this damn telephone; it's behaving like a maniac at the moment.'

As though to reproach me, it rang again.

As Sebastian had recently had occasion to remark, the telephone wires were the veins through which our life's blood flowed, and, to assist the healthy circulation as far as possible, I had had an extension installed on practically every flat surface in the house, including the sideboard. Now, at the first hesitant ping, I fell upon it like a drowning sailor.

This time it really was Julian, but, even if I had remembered to put on the disguised voice, it could hardly have deepened the confusion. My first reaction was that his old friend Peregrine had caught up with him, in no uncertain manner. His voice was so thick and blurred that I could scarcely hear what he said, let alone make sense of it.

'Tesha, Tesha! Tha'you, Tesha? Oh God ... gotta warn you ... for ... Tesha ... hearme?'

'What's happened? What's the matter?'

'Bad ... Gemme doc ... Barnes ... no Barnes ...'

'What is it? Are you ill?'

'Hurt .. I'm hur ... tha'key ... unnerstan ... ?'

'Don't worry about that now. Try and tell me what's happened.'

'Bad ... you got help ... you know ... elp ... elp ...'

His voice trailed away. There was a sound of coughing, then a faint thud; after that, silence.

I went on shouting his name, but nothing happened, so gave up at last and went slowly back to my seat.

Sandy stared across the table at me, her eyes popping: 'Something up, old lady?'

'I'm not sure. Somebody having a joke, probably.'

'How beastly! Scared you, too, hasn't it? Better let me take the calls now, in case the joker tries it on again.'

'I have a feeling he won't,' I replied, not quite knowing why I said it. 'It was Julian Brown, actually, and I'm afraid he's in no condition to talk sensibly about jobs or anything else. At first, I thought he was stoned, but then he seemed to be trying to warn me about something, and that's not the way it takes drunks as a rule, is it?'

'Couldn't say, m'dear. Haven't had much experience in that line. Warning you about what?'

'I honestly can't tell you. It was all so indistinct, and finally he more or less passed out. Can he have been ill, or was it just a feeble joke? I do wish I knew.'

'Well, now, let's put our heads together,' Sandy said, blessedly matter of fact, as usual. 'Why not give him a tinkle? Do you know the number?'

'It's a private one, separate from the shop. Wait a bit, though. It rings in the Boardroom, too. Barnes might know something.'

'The very ticket! Can you remember the number?'

'It's in my diary,' I said. 'Wherever that may be.'

'Well, you sit still and I'll trot along and find it. You're looking pretty washed out.'

She was gone only a few minutes, which I spent staring wretchedly at my plate, trying to shake off a fearful apprehension.

'Eureka!' Sandy whooped, bursting into the room again and waving my diary. 'I'll make the call for you, shall I?'

'If you like. What's the time?'

'Ten after two.'

'Then Barnes won't be back yet. We'd better wait.'

'Well, no harm in having a go, is there? I hate to see you in the dumps and experience has taught me that action is generally the best cure for that. We'll probably find there's a perfectly simple explanation and have a good laugh about it.'

'Very well,' I said, and read out the number.

She dialled it and stood waiting, with a smile of encouragement, which only very slowly faded:

'No answer was the stern reply,' she said at last.

'Oh damn!'

'Not to worry; I'll hang on a bit. Somebody may hear.'

Apparently no one did, for her patience was unrewarded. Still watching me, her hand hovered uncertainly over the instrument, before the receiver came to rest, sympathy and concern radiating from her moon-like face.

'Something is terribly wrong,' I said.

'Oh, I say! Hold your horses! What makes you so sure?'

'I don't know, but it was like a great, black wave, sweeping over me.'

'Ah! these volatile, artistic temperaments! Up in the air, one minute, down in the depths the next. It would never do for me. Whenever I'm on a sticky wicket, the best medicine I know is to get to grips with it. So, how about cudgelling the old brains? You might find yourself remembering something to give us a lead as to where Mr B was, when he rang you. But, look here, I don't want to barge in, if it upsets you.'

'No, it was your calling him Mr B which made me jump. That's another story. Now, please do eat something, while I tell you what he said. Perhaps you'll have one of your brainwaves.'

At the end of my brief recital, she said thoughtfully: 'It sounds to me as though your first theory was right. He'd been on the binge and had a couple over the eight. If so, he could have been anywhere. He doesn't sound the sort to go in for solitary boozing.'

'He doesn't go in much for any kind of boozing, solitary or otherwise.'

'Ah well, we all have our occasional falls by the wayside. And I feel sure that's the answer, honour bright! Now, what time did you say this chap, Barnes, would be back?'

'Not till after three.'

'So only half an hour to wait. We should be able to keep on an even keel till then, don't you think?'

It was more than was required of us, however. Just before the time was up, Robin came, in person, to break the news for which I was already half prepared, and to soothe me out of a shock which I had not even the heart to simulate.

Twelve

Unlike Sandy, who had exhorted me to keep a stiff upper lip, Robin seemed quite put out by the fatalistic calm with which I received his shattering news, although paying me the doubtful compliment of attributing this to obtuseness, rather than want of feeling. He flatly refused to accept my composure as genuine.

'Look, darling, I'm so afraid this is going to hit you badly, when it sinks in. Do sit down quietly, and let me fetch some brandy for your poor nerves.'

'No, the time for that has passed. I've known, for at least an hour, that Julian was dead.'

'Oh, come now! That would put you ahead even of the one who found the body. We don't want that sort of talk.'

'Who was it?'

'Who was what, my love?'

'The one who found him?'

He ignored this, saying anxiously: 'It is a fact, isn't it, that you've been indoors ever since one-thirty or so? You didn't go out again?'

'No, of course not. It was the telephone call, you see.'

'Yes, tell me about that.'

I did so, adding: 'I realise now that he must actually have been dying. I feel so awful that I did nothing to help him, just tried to tell myself he was drunk. And yet, you know, Robin, the moment he rang off, I had these terrible forebodings. I can't explain why, but, when we tried to call him back, something told me that he was dead.'

Robin, having a congenital distrust of words like foreboding, automatically tossed these valuable presentiments to the winds: 'You must try not to over-dramatise it. Just think back and see if there's one tiny point you've forgotten to tell me.'

'In my own words, I suppose?' I said acidly, for I was beginning to resent the ease with which he had slipped into the role of cross-examiner, confronted by the half-baked witness.

'No, in his, preferably.'

On the third run through, I considered myself word perfect, but had reckoned without Sandy:

'Hang on, old dear! Haven't you left out something about a key?'

The omission had been only partly accidental, but Sandy was naturally unaware of this, so I pretended to be grateful:

'Quite right. He was trying to warn me, as I've told you, and then I think he said: "the key, the key," but his voice was so blurred that it was difficult to pick out individual words. He might have been saying the bee, or the fee, for all I know. Oh dear, if only he'd had the sense to tell me who'd attacked him, instead of burbling on about unimportant things, how much better it would have been!'

It was not until several days later that I realised how unjustified was this complaint. In fact, as I knew later, and almost too late, in that brief, incoherent telephone call, Julian had given me the best clue he possessed to the identity, not only of his murderer, but of Mr B, as well.

Robin, however, being equally unaware of such things, fastened on my words: 'How do you know it was so unimportant? What key could he have meant? Any idea at all?'

Even as he asked me, I saw I could deny it. Until then, I had naturally assumed that the key in question was the one to our alcove cupboard; but, all at once, I recalled talk of another key, or rather set of keys, which blasted my previous notions, and put me almost as much in the dark as I had pretended to be: 'A possible explanation,' I said, 'is that he was referring to the key of the lift."

I described the system at Thurgoods for sealing off the Boardroom to unauthorised visitors, during Barnes's absence, which, in view of the timing of Julian's call, could have had great significance, and Sandy, at any rate, found this interpretation acceptable.

'Great Scot, yes!' she said excitedly. 'Trust you to hit the nail on the head! He was trying to tell you that someone had got hold of a lift key, and had sneaked upstairs, when he knew the place would be deserted. The very ticket!'

'It could be,' Robin said dubiously. 'No accounting for the sort of obsession that would take hold of a man, in those extremities, but it doesn't make a lot of sense. You seem certain it was you he was trying to warn, and yet one can hardly see why a stolen lift key should put you in any danger. You're sure he wasn't trying to say something else? Like someone's name, for instance?'

'No, Barnes was the only name he mentioned. First of all, he mumbled something about getting a doctor, and then he said: "No, Barnes".'

'It might have been "know", with a k, I suppose? Asking if you knew who he meant?'

'Yes, it might, but that would make even less sense. Anyway, Robin, we've told you absolutely everything, and now it's your turn. What exactly happened, and how did you get on to it so quickly?'

He hesitated, then glanced up in alarm, as Sandy exploded into ostentatious coughing. It was not a seizure, however, but a subtle reminder of her presence, and she said awkwardly: 'Perhaps I should be tanking off? No offence, I mean, but you two might prefer a parlez-vous on your ownsome?'

'Oh, don't go,' I said. 'Your moral support may be needed, and I bet you're just as curious as I am. You needn't worry about his giving away any secrets. I'm the last one he'll tell them to.'

'Oh, I can't quite swallow that, old girl.'

'It's true, none the less,' Robin said. 'And can you blame me? In any case, I can only tell you what you'll both be reading in the papers, in an hour or two. They'll play it up for all it's worth, I daresay: "Millionaire Playboy", "West End Club Man", "Friend of Princess Margaret" stabbed to death. Take your pick.'

'Stabbed?' Sandy repeated, in horror. 'Was he really?'

'I'm afraid so. From behind. He was sitting at his desk.'

'So it has to be murder? No question of suicide, or accident?'

'None. It's not my case, but I can say that much with absolute certainty.'

'If it's not your case,' I asked, 'how come you know so much about it?'

'Sheer fluke. The local branch called us in, and a mate of mine is working on it. He happened to remember reading in some gossip column that you'd been seen lunching with Julian Brown, and he thought I might be interested.'

'So you haven't actually seen the ... Julian, I mean?'

'Yes, I have. My first idea was to get down here and give you the news, before you heard it from anyone else; then, at the last minute, I decided to drop in at Thurgoods first. I knew you'd be clamouring for the details.'

'I don't seem to have got many. Have they any idea who did it?'

'No. Whoever it was, he or she was not considerate enough to remain on the scene, nor even to leave the weapon behind.'

'Who found him? Not Barnes?'

'Oh? Why not him?'

'Because, if he did, there's some hanky panky. He doesn't normally go back to the shop until the pub closes, at three.'

'Hanky panky is an understatement, but, in fact, it wasn't he.'

'Who, then?'

'Brace yourself; it was your friend, Betty.'

Sandy gave an involuntary exclamation; then put a hand to her mouth. I concealed my own emotions with more expertise.

'Poor old Betty,' I said casually. 'What a ghastly shock for her! Was she dreadfully upset?'

'Not so's you'd notice; but, then, she's quite a tough nut, isn't she?'

'She's not the kind to swoon, or to go into hysterics, if that's what you mean.'

'Strangely enough, that is exactly what I mean. She was calm and coherent, and she confined herself to the bare facts, which was all that was required. She has her wits about her,' he added thoughtfully, and, knowing something of masculine prejudice in this sphere, I said: 'Wits enough to have removed herself twenty miles from the scene, if she had anything to hide. Was he already dead, when she found him?'

'So she says.'

'What time was that?'

'A little after two, I gather.'

'Then it can only have been just after I spoke to him. Oh, poor Julian! To think he must literally have been dying then, Sandy! Oh, if only we'd done something; got a doctor for him, or something.'

'It wouldn't have done the slightest good; I can promise you that, so please don't torture yourself unnecessarily. I've got to be off now, but perhaps Sandy can stay with you for a bit?'

'There's no need. Besides, Bobs will be worrying, and we can't have that.'

Robin looked as though he could have had it, with no trouble at all, but a gleam of relief spread over Sandy's face. Even the thrill of being practically in at the death, so to speak, could not dim her grinding responsibility to the remorseless old Bobs.

'I don't want to leave the sinking ship, chaps, but I'll just give a buzz on the old blower, to see if things are on an even keel, if that's all right with you?'

'Use my bedroom extension,' I advised her, knowing what a wigging was probably in store for her, and wishing to spare her the embarrassment of submitting to it in our presence.

'Talking of telephone calls,' Robin said, when she had gone. 'They may send someone round to get a statement from you about the one from Julian. I know Sandy would back you to the hilt, in any flummery, but do try to be as truthful and accurate as you can, will you?'

I looked pained: 'Really, Robin! As though I would lie about a thing like that!'

'Well, perhaps that was putting it too strongly. I know you wouldn't falsify anything deliberately, but you are apt to forget to draw a line between fact and fiction, and it's important to remember that any exaggerations or embroideries would be more likely to help the murderer than anyone else. I suppose you wouldn't want that to happen?'

'A lot would depend on who he was.'

'Would it, indeed? You mean, you would actually cover up for a friend, even if you believed he or she had killed someone?'

This was dangerous ground, and I said hastily: 'No, of course not, darling. It's only when you treat me like a half-wit that I make these feeble jokes. I couldn't possibly want to stay friends with a murderer, could I?'

'I can't decide whether it's your logic, or your moral code that I find most confusing,' Robin said sadly, 'but I haven't time to work it out now. Are you sure you're all right? Perhaps Sandy will be able to stay for a bit?'

'Perhaps,' I said absently, for my thoughts were on a new tack. For the past ten minutes, an unspoken question of such sizzling properties had lain between us that I had not dared to bring it into the open. Only the prospect of his leaving me with it still unanswered gave me the courage to say:

'By the way, what was Betty doing on the second floor, at two in the afternoon?'

Robin had been halfway to the door, but he turned and came towards me again: 'Does that strike you as odd?'

'Oh dear me, no; not odd at all, far from it; but she is a bit of a stickler for her two-hour lunch-break, as a rule. I'm sure she had a million reasons for being on the premises today, though.'

'She may have had. Would you be interested to hear the one she gave us?'

'I would, rather.'

'She said she had lost a customer.'

'Lost one?'

'So she said. She had lost a customer and was looking for him on the second floor.'

'Then it must be true, though it does sound a bit careless.'

'It appears that she took a client up to the Boardroom, in accordance with that quaint custom you once described to me; but, as there were some other people there, whom she personally disliked, she only stayed for a couple of minutes. He, the customer, that is, was to have been given a drink, before the bar closed, and then returned to Betty, to finish off the transaction. She waited on her floor for about twenty minutes, but he didn't come back. Being rather anxious about the deal, she went in search of him. The lift door was locked, by then, but she had her own key. Barnes had gone, and so had the customer. Her theory is that he changed his mind about buying the thing, but hadn't the guts to tell her so, and skipped out, while her back was turned. Unfortunately, she hadn't got as far as collecting his name and address, and it was the first time he'd been in the shop, so we may have a little difficulty in tracing him. She also says that the door of Julian's office was ajar, so she had looked inside, on the remote chance that he had gone in there.'

'Well, you won't even need to trace him,' I said, 'because I can vouch for the first part of the story. They came up to the Boardroom together, just before I left.'

'What time was that?'

'Fifty-five minutes before the first race at Epsom, if you want it exact.'

'I believe you, though thousands wouldn't. And I do implore you, Tessa, not to give that kind of reply to the Sergeant. He'd probably suspect you of sending him up, which wouldn't do at all.'

'And nothing could be further from my intentions, but I am not in the habit of consulting my watch every five minutes, on the off chance that murders are about to be committed in the vicinity. On the other hand, Barnes had just had occasion to point out that the first race was due to start in an hour, and I can promise you that he is an expert in these matters.'

'I'll take your word for it, but tell me exactly what happened, so far as your own knowledge goes.'

Numerous reasons delayed my response to this one. There was the thought that Sandy must be going through a hell of a session with Bobs, to have stayed away so long; plus a faint irritation over Robin's trick of falling into police jargon, whenever he asked me a simple question. However, I did not speak of these matters, nor ask him how I could be expected to tell of things which were outside my own knowledge because still another diversionary factor was the ominous sound of creakings and rustlings from the passage, signifying the presence of an eavesdropper. I concluded that Sebastian had stationed himself outside the door, and I was determined that whatever else he might overhear it should not include a domestic tiff. So I described the incident, just as it had occurred, of Betty's arrival upstairs, with her customer in tow.

It was discouraging to find that at least one of my listeners was unconvinced. I could tell, from Robin's sceptical look, that he wondered that such a brief tale should have been prefaced by such a weighty pause.

'There were three other witnesses,' I said defensively. 'And I haven't invented the whole thing, just to back up Betty, whatever you may think.'

'No, of course, you wouldn't be so foolish; and, as it

happens, Barnes has already given the same version. He also says that the three people went down in the lift together, about ten minutes after you did. Julian had still not returned, by then, so I doubt if you'll be asked about that part of it. It's the telephone call they'll concentrate on. Luckily, Sandy was present, and will be able to stop you going too far off the rails.'

'Someone taking my name in vain?' she asked, putting her head round the door. 'Is this a private conflab, or may one barge in?'

'Barge away,' I told her. 'The witness was just being coached, but we've got it straight now. How's Bobs?'

'Not too dusty, I'm happy to say. Hope I didn't speak out of turn, but I had to give just the weeniest hint of what was afoot. Anyway, it did the trick. I'm to stay for as long as I'm needed, if you please!'

'We do please,' Robin said. 'And are duly grateful. I'll try and get back early, but stay with her as long as you can.'

'Count on me, m'dear.'

'When do we not? Goodbye, then, darling.'

'Oh, goodbye, my love,' I said abstractedly. I had been seized by an impulse, during their back slapping little exchange, and, eager to act on it with all speed, I turned to Sandy as soon as we were alone, saying: 'Wait here a moment, will you? I am just going to tell Sebastian to toddle out for one of his breathers, and then I'll be back. There is something I want to consult you about, and it is essential not to be overheard.'

'Fire away!' she said, when I returned.

Despite the prod, I did not begin at once, for it behoved me to take my time. I sat quietly in my chair, gazing sombrely at the alcove cupboard, and then I fired my opening round.

'Look here, Sandy, in a hypothetical manner of

speaking, if there was a red-hot secret, known to only two people in the entire world, and one of them unexpectedly died, would you say that the person who was left alive had a moral obligation to go to the grave with that secret, or not?'

Sandy was equally deliberate, and the hypothetical question received its due weight. Luckily, the answer, when at last forthcoming, was exactly the one I had been seeking.

Thirteen

Not being officially assigned to Julian's case, Robin felt free to discuss it in rather more expansive terms than would otherwise have been possible, and to keep me informed of developments. Unfortunately, these were meagre, almost to the point of non-existence. In the six hours following the crime, only two significant facts had been established. One was that death had been caused by a knife wound, inflicted from behind by someone standing up; the other was the approximate time of death. Neither the weapon, nor any hint of a motive had turned up, far less any clue to the murderer's identity.

The last item brought a relief for which I gave much thanks, for, once the initial shock of Julian's death had worn off, I soon began to see what a sticky wicket Betty had chosen to bat on. The unlucky combination of having been first on the scene, and her outrageously improbable story to account for it must have struck even the most lenient of detectives as worthy of investigation. All this, in addition to her somewhat equivocal behaviour in recent weeks, had placed her, so far as I was concerned, in a highly vulnerable position, and it was soothing to discover that the police did not share this view. Robin flatly denied that an arrest was imminent, or even contemplated.

'What is the official theory, then? I suppose they have one?'

'Half a dozen, probably; but nothing to substantiate any of them.'

'Not even the good old escaped prisoner, who's doing ten years for robbery with violence?'

'Least of all him. This wasn't the work of some thug who lost his head. It was an expert job, performed by someone who knew exactly where to put the knife in. Besides, nothing was stolen.'

'What?' I asked, startled. 'How do you know?'

'I don't absolutely know, but they found wads of cash in his pockets, not to mention a gold cigarette case and lighter.'

'Any keys?'

'Ah! The key motif again! Yes, plenty, as a matter of fact. Car keys; latch key and mortice, both belonging to the house; and a separate bunch of shop keys. However, it's an odd coincidence, in view of what he said to you.'

'What is?'

'As I say, the shop keys were on a separate ring and, for a time, that special one for the lift did appear to be missing. Great excitement all round, as you can imagine. However, it soon turned up.'

'Where?'

'Under the desk, but tucked away, near the window. The theory is that it must have fallen out of his pocket, at some point, and, in jerking his foot, perhaps when the blow was struck, he had contrived to kick it away. Whether that had any connection with what he was trying to tell you is still a mystery.'

'And it doesn't rule out the possibility of his having come back to the office unexpectedly and found the murderer in the act of pinching something. That's quite logical, in view of the time he was killed.'

'Highly logical. The only snag is that, as I say, nothing is missing, and if the unknown intruder had gone to the extreme lengths of committing murder to get what he came for, one could hardly conceive of his being so frivolous as to leave without it.'

'But how do you know he did leave without it? I should have thought only Julian could tell you that, and perhaps he was killed simply to prevent his doing so? Your actual motive, in fact.'

'It's a neat idea, but it doesn't tie in with the evidence.'

'Whose evidence?'

'No less than his three closest relatives; presumably the people in the best position to know, since they shared a house, as well as a business.'

'And they all had the nerve to say there was nothing missing?'

'I don't know about nerve, but that's what they claim. It seems that he only used this particular office as a kind of social headquarters. He kept his engagement diary in there, a few personal papers, and so forth, but all the business files and correspondence were in the office next door. Well, you know all this already, Tessa. It was you who first told me about this weird, schizophrenic life of his.'

'Yes, but there was one thing I didn't tell you. Now, please don't be fierce. It had no special importance at the time, and I daresay it still hasn't. It's only the fact that all three of those sharks have denied its existence that makes me feel it might have a bearing.'

'Could you possibly tell me what you're talking about?'

'I am talking about a ten-volume, intimate, personal and madly indiscreet diary, which Julian has spent the last twenty years compiling. That office, in actual fact, was the author's sanctum. If none of them has noticed the diary is missing, they're either blind, or lying through their teeth. I'll give you one guess as to the explanation I favour.'

'But, darling, what makes you so sure that it is missing?'

I told him, in a few well-chosen words. I left out irrelevant matters, such as the elusive Jasmine, but made great play of the family's bitter opposition to the diary's publication, and of Mrs Teddy's crude attempts to thwart it, which had brought it to its eventual hiding place.

'So, you see,' I concluded, 'it would really be too staggering a coincidence if the very thing they had all been so steamed up about had vanished, without one of them noticing the fact.'

'It certainly introduces a new element,' Robin said. 'And I do think you might have told me all this before.'

'I meant to, really I did, but how could I have foreseen that he would be murdered before I got around to it?'

'Nevertheless, since he has been, it is a trifle disconcerting to find that a bundle of evidence is reposing on my own premises.'

'I realise that, and I could kick myself for allowing him to bring it here. But it was only intended as a stopgap. I told him he was to remove it at the earliest possible moment, and I'd have nagged him till he did. Anyway, that's not the worst of it.'

'Oh Lord! Surely you can't have anything worse up your sleeve? Go carefully, because I may easily faint.'

'Put yourself in my shoes, and you'll soon see which one of us has the best right to faint. Can't you imagine how I've been plaguing myself with the idea that, if only I'd defied him, and broadcast to all and sundry where the diary was hidden, he might have outlived us all?'

'Then I suggest you stop plaguing yourself right now. It presupposes, does it not, that he returned to his office unexpectedly, found someone ransacking it, and was killed because he refused to say where the diary was hidden?'

'Yes, and I am afraid it's the obvious solution.'

'Well, I'm not. Nothing in his office had been disturbed; there was no struggle, and he'd made no attempt to defend himself. On the contrary, he was sitting at his desk, which, as you'll remember, takes up nearly the whole width of the office. His assailant would necessarily have been stationed behind him, and I cannot believe that a man would quietly turn his back on someone whom he'd just discovered rifling his office. The natural thing, even if he didn't know the fellow had a knife, would have been to send him packing, or open the door and yell for help.'

'It wouldn't have been any use. Barnes was off duty and there wouldn't have been another soul up there, during the lunch hour.'

'So we assume that the murderer timed it deliberately like that, and, ergo, was someone with an intimate knowledge of the routine?'

'Unfortunately, it's a well-populated field. The set-up is well known to two people, to my certain knowledge. There may be dozens more.'

'All the same, whether the murderer was someone Julian knew well, or only slightly, it doesn't explain his breaking off the argument, to sit down at his desk, while the adversary was still in the room.'

'Why not? If he didn't know the man was armed, why shouldn't he have turned his back at that point? Listen!' I stood up. 'Listen to this, Robin! Imaginary dialogue:

'Julian: "Get out."

'Murderer: "No."
'Julian: "Then I'll throw you out."
'Murderer: "You and who else, ha ha, etcetera."
'Julian: "I'll call the police, if you don't leave."
'Murderer: "Go ahead and call them, ha ha."'

I had used different voices for this dramatic reconstruction, plus some graphic miming, and ended up with my hand on the telephone, my back half turned to Robin. He fell into the spirit of the thing, advancing stealthily, to dig his cigarette lighter into my ribs, uttering a final villainous 'Ha Ha!' as he withdrew his hand. Whereupon, I collapsed across the table, sobbing like a fool.

'Oh, I'm dreadfully sorry, Tessa. I didn't mean to hurt you, and it was only a weeny tap.'

'Not that,' I blubbered. 'Not hurt. It's just that I made it all so real for myself, and it wasn't funny any more. Sounds silly, but I actually became Julian for a split second, when you jabbed me with that thing. I felt a terrible, searing pain in my heart, and I knew that I was dying.'

'Poor old love! But you'll feel better, now you've had a good bellow,' Robin said dispassionately. 'I knew you'd reach this stage, sooner or later. It's a good thing to have got it over.'

His nannyish tones pulled me together in a trice, and, not caring to have my hypersensitivity dismissed so casually, I said: 'I am not so confident that it is over.'

'In that case, let's drop the subject. No point in distressing yourself. Come on, now! Wipe your nose and straighten your false eyelashes, and I'll take you out to dinner.'

'I don't feel like it. Besides, I couldn't go in this,' I said, looking dismally at the pink trouser suit, which I had not bothered to change, and realising that now

I could never wear it again: 'Anyway, what did you think of my death scene? It could have happened like that, couldn't it?'

'It's conceivable. The telephone was dangling off the hook when they found him, which adds a bit of weight.'

'There! That practically proves it. Oh my God, Robin!'

'What now?'

'Well, don't you see? It must have been me he was telephoning. Not the police; me!'

'Yes, almost certainly, I should say.'

'Why didn't you say so before? I feel worse than ever now.'

'And well you might; though I doubt if you've quite grasped the spot it puts you in.'

'What spot?'

'I've been reluctant to mention it, but perhaps forewarned is forearmed. Hasn't it struck you that, if the murderer overheard any of that telephone call, he would put two and two together. Can't you see the danger to yourself?'

'No, I hadn't quite grasped it,' I admitted. 'And, I must say, you're taking it very calmly. You seem to have reconciled yourself to the situation with unflattering speed.'

'No purpose would be served by getting in a stew, but I am far from reconciled, I assure you. Various counter measures come to mind, and it's some consolation that our premise is based on a hypothetical set of facts. The murderer may well have believed that death would be instantaneous, and have been out of earshot when Julian called you.'

'I sincerely hope so, but, even if old hypothesis turns out to be right, there's not all that much risk, is there? I mean, assuming that Julian was killed in order to stop publication of the diaries, that would be the end of it, surely? Even if the murderer does suspect they're hidden here, he wouldn't be such a fool as to try knocking me off just to get his hands on them. He must know that I'd pass them over without a murmur.'

'It's not quite as simple as that, you know. Somehow, I don't visualise him stepping up to the front door, raising his hat and politely requesting you to produce the diaries.'

'Why not? I'd do it like a shot.'

'Wouldn't it also occur to you to take a look at him?'

'Well, naturally ... Oh, I see what you mean!'

'It might even enter your mind to ring up the police, and tell them about it. Perhaps, being you, you'd do nothing of the kind, but I fancy that is what he would expect of you.'

I could see the force of this, and was obliged to admit that my brain had been ticking over rather sluggishly, in requiring it to be spelt out for me.

'I'm afraid I'm still a bit confused. What's your guess, then? That he'll stage a burglary, one evening, when we're all out?'

'Hardly. It won't take him long to discover that the house is a perfect web of alarms, all connected with the local station. I don't underestimate him, and I imagine he'd try a smarter dodge than that.'

'What's to be done, then?'

'It's more a question of what not to do, at this stage. Like repeating these theories of ours outside this room; and certainly not telling a soul where the diaries are hidden. How many know about that already, by the way?'

'Two. Three, at the most,' I said.

'Ah!'

'Not "Ah" at all. You and I are two. It makes three, if

the murderer got it out of Julian, before he killed him.'

'And no one else?'

'Cross my heart.'

'Not even Sandy? Careful, now!'

'Not even Sandy. I had intended to include her. In fact, it was on her advice that I've told you. Then, I thought that would be enough to be going on with.'

'Good! The fewer who know, the better.'

'Do you really think so? I would have thought there might have been safety in numbers. However, you're the expert, so we'll play it your way. Anyway, you know everything now, which is all that matters. It's a load off my mind. The murderer will guess that I've told you, and that you'd be on to him in a flash if he tried any tricks.'

'And you're sure that it really is everything? Not a single detail left out?'

'Oh! Oh well, to be perfectly frank, there is just one other tiny thing. Now, please don't frown at me like that, Robin. I only discovered it myself a few hours ago, and it literally went out of my head until this moment.'

'Well? What was it?'

'You remember that we agreed, last night, to hang on to the book carrier, pending further developments?'

'Yes, of course.'

'And you know that I packed it up and put the box away in my wardrobe? You saw me do that?'

'With my own eyes.'

'I feared as much,' I said sadly. 'I was afraid I couldn't have forgotten, so soon, where it was hidden.'

'You don't mean to say, Tessa ... ?'

'Yes, I do. I don't suppose it's the slightest bit relevant, but by lunch-time today it had gone; vanished; scarpered, as Sandy would say.'

Fourteen

We spent a quiet weekend, with no disguised encyclopaedia salesmen or spurious book-carrier collectors attempting to break and enter, and were recovering from the slight anti-climax of this on Sunday evening when Betty telephoned.

My immediate fear was that she intended to pump me about police progress on the murder case, so I assumed my guarded look. She could not see it, of course, but a suitable expression often helps to conjure up the right words and a matching tone of voice.

These tactics were superfluous, however, for she began by saying: 'Are you doing anything special tomorrow?'

Rearranging my features, I confessed that I was not.

'Care for a spin in the country?'

'Aren't you working?' I asked, playing for time.

'That's no answer, is it? I'm not, as it happens. They're closing down until after the funeral. That's family only, so I'm not expected to attend.'

'What about the inquest? Isn't that tomorrow?'

'Yes, I have to say my piece there, but it's at ten o'clock, and a pure formality, so they tell me. It'll take about ten minutes, and then they adjourn. Not that it makes it any less macabre. That's partly why I'd like to get away for a bit, as soon as it's over.'

'Partly?'

'Yes, I'll explain the rest of it when we're on the open road. That is, if you mean to come.'

'Oh, sure! Anything for a change!'

'That's the spirit. Do you think we'd stand a chance of getting tickets for Stratford?'

'So that's where we're heading, is it? No, I shouldn't think so for a moment.'

'Still, it might be worth trying. You probably know someone there who could wangle it for us?'

'Depends. What are they doing tomorrow?'

'Hamlet, I think.'

'Oh, bother! I've seen that.'

'Ha, ha, very funny! What do you think, really?'

'Less than nothing, frankly. There's no matinee on Monday.'

'I know that, fathead. I thought we might stay the night.'

'Oh, did you? And have you already made hotel reservations?'

'Provisionally. Any objection?'

'No, but I'll have to ask Robin. He may have some.'

'Call me back, when you've talked to him. Not too late, though, because I mean to treat myself to an early night.'

'Okay, but there's one other thing. He's bound to ask where I'm staying. What's the address of these provisional hotel rooms?'

'You can ring him up, when you get there. We may decide not to stay, after all.'

It was always amusing, in a mean-spirited sort of way, to spike Betty's guns when she imagined she was getting away with something, and I regretted not being able to see her go toppling off her perch, as I said gaily: 'Oh, come on, it's quite safe. The address won't mean a thing to Robin. He's never even heard of Jasmine Hawkes.'

(ii)

'How did you track her down?' I asked, as we slowed down at the approaches to stately Beaconsfield.

It was a fair distance to have covered with the burning question still unspoken, but we had devoted the first hour of the journey to the inquest, which had turned out much as Betty had predicted.

Evidence had been given by a Superintendent, the old gossip column addict, in person, no doubt, and Mr Brown had formally identified the remains as those of his son, Arthur Edwin Brown, also known as Julian of that ilk.

Betty claimed to have been shocked by his bearing, which, in three days, had deteriorated into that of a feeble old man. He had been on the verge of collapse in the witness box, and his muttered responses had been inaudible to most of the courtroom. The Coroner had treated him gently, only once urging him to speak up.

'Genuine, or putting it on a bit?' I had asked.

'He'd need to be a bloody good actor, and I don't see it, somehow. They were a very tight little family, you know, in spite of all the rows, and it's not a particularly nice thing to happen to any father.'

'I agree, but he's not just any father, is he? For one thing, his attitude to death doesn't follow quite the normal pattern.'

'All that spiritualism, you mean?'

'Yes. The impression Julian gave me was that he was completely hooked on it. Apparently it was his wife's death which started him off on that caper.'

'Well, I don't know about that; but, however devoutly he may believe that his son is now in a better world, murder is hardly the means he would have chosen to despatch him there. He's rather a soft-hearted old party, as it happens. Unpretentious, too. I think he'd have been quite content to potter along, in a modest way, if the younger generation hadn't been so set on turning him into a tycoon. I daresay he was out of his depth in this world, and consoled himself by dreaming up contacts with the next one.'

This indicated a more lovable personality than the old villain of Julian's diary, but I recalled that it was through Brown senior that Betty had landed her job at Thurgoods, and that she was possibly somewhat biased.

'At any rate,' I said, 'it is to be hoped that the experience has had a chastening effect on both of them. Otherwise some very tart remarks will be flying back and forth across the Great Divide.'

Overtaking a Mini car, three saloons and a caravan in one grim and purposeful swoop, Betty said sharply: 'You're pretty callous, I must say. I thought Julian was a friend of yours?'

'Well, an old acquaintance, really, and in no danger of being forgot; but it would be sheer hypocrisy to pretend that he and his father were on good terms, when we both know that they hated the sight of each other. I'm not suggesting that the old boy was responsible in any way, but I do think it's a bit thick to pretend that he's broken-hearted.'

She did not deign to reply to this. We had become enmeshed in some gargantuan road-works in the purlieus of Gerrards Cross, and all her spleen was reserved for the follies of the Ministry of Transport, and criminal lunacy of other drivers, who were sneaking up a good deal faster in their lanes than we were in ours.

Even when released from these toils her disapproval of them, or possibly myself, smouldered on, and we covered the next three or four miles at a cracking speed. It was not until the sobering effect of the aforementioned Beaconsfield had slackened the pace to something compatible with sanity that I had ventured to embark on the subject of Jasmine.

Instead of answering, she said abruptly: 'Shall we stop for a drink at one of these quaint hostelries? We could work out our route and decide where to have lunch.'

Without troubling to procure my consent, she shot into a space between two parked cars, severely ruffling the nerves of a gangling golden retriever, who had marked out that section of the gutter for purposes of his own.

'You don't care for dogs?' I inquired, opening my door, as the creature pounded frantically down the road.

'They're all right, in their place.'

'Like attached by a lead to a customer? Less likely to get lost?'

The question was not entirely artless, and she paid me out by slamming on the hand-brake with such violence that, in the act of stepping out of the car, I practically tipped forward, nose first, on to the pavement. She emerged from her side and stalked ahead of me into the Crown and Anchor, or whatever it was called.

Pausing in the dim interior, which was illuminated on this fine May morning by twenty-watt yellow bulbs, in the two eighteenth-century-type coach lamps, Betty glanced around, then strode off to the Ladies.

I groped my way to a vacant table through a smothering collection of horse brasses and copper warming pans, and came to rest in a brown corduroy G Plan chair, *circa* 1950.

There were three red-faced men at the next table,

drinking Scotch and discussing motor cars in technical yet passionate terms, which I found completely riveting, though I cannot imagine why. I feel sure that, had they pulled their chairs round and started talking at me about motor cars, straining my ears to listen would have been the last thing I should have thought of doing.

Betty joined me, and, seating herself in the twin G Plan, announced: 'As a matter of fact it was like falling off a log; no trouble at all.'

'Oh, good!' I said vaguely.

'For God's sake, wake up, Tessa. Dammit all, you're the one who was so keen to know how I found her address.'

'Oh, sorry. I hadn't connected. The compulsive fascination of gaskets and spark plugs had me in its grip. Of course, I'm dying to hear. Fire away, as Sandy says.'

'I've just told you, there was nothing to it. I simply asked her where she was living and she told me.'

This was news, indeed, and I rewarded her with my full attention and many a Fancy That!

'I wonder why neither of us ever thought of that before? I suppose we got bogged down by the silly idea that we couldn't ask her for her address until we knew where she was. How did you overcome the problem?'

'She rang me up.'

'No kidding?'

'None. It was on Sunday, just before I spoke to you. She'd seen the announcement of Julian's murder and was agog.'

'How very peculiar!'

'My dear child, if you'd spent the past forty-eight hours in my flat, you wouldn't think so. The number of dear friends who rang up to commiserate, and then fished for the gruesome details, would astonish you.'

'No, it wouldn't; but, all the same, there is something peculiar about Hawkes getting on the bandwagon. She, who went to such pains to keep her whereabouts secret.'

'Has it struck you that she might only have been anxious to do so, while Julian was alive?'

'Why would that be?'

'Well, you know what he was like? Every whim became an obsession. He'd never have given her any peace once he'd found her.'

'That's true, but if there's such a tame explanation, why are we both slogging off now to call on her?'

'I'd better go and get our drinks at the bar,' Betty said. 'They obviously don't intend to serve us here. What do you want?'

I told her, and she traipsed off. My three red-faced friends were still at it, but the thrill had gone. If they had driven their cars in top gear all the way to the summit of Mount Everest, I should hardly have cocked a languid ear, so absorbed was I in Betty's news. There was more in it than met the eye, was what I told myself.

She returned, with two glasses, and, not being one to waste a graphic phrase, I said: 'There is more in this than meets the eye.'

She downed a double measure of gin, and some of her truculence seemed to evaporate with it. She grinned and said: 'Well, it's your own fault, if you feel you've been led up the garden a bit. You sometimes pretend to be more stupid than you are.'

'I suppose your plan was that I should tag along as chaperone and map reader, until you pulled up at some pub and said: "My, what a funny coincidence! Can that be Jasmine Hawkes behind the bar?"'

'Why not? It wouldn't have done you any harm, and,

after all, this is a purely private hare I'm pursuing.'

'Private or not, you've got me involved up to my neck, so you'd better come clean. I've no desire to be less stupid than I am for two whole days at a stretch, but I warn you that I will, if I have to.'

'I have a personal reason for wanting to get in touch with Jasmine, and, when she telephoned out of the blue, I asked her for her address, and she made the most frightful bloomer.'

'You mean, she told you?'

'No, she said she wouldn't be back there until this morning. You know how people are apt to assume that the other person can tell where they're calling from? Until then, I'd taken it for granted that she was in the country, but the mere fact of being in London was enough to make her believe that I knew it, too.'

'And did you, by any chance, discover how long she'd been there?'

'You bet. It was almost worthy of you. I pretended that I'd known it all along, and I said it was a great coincidence because I had an idea I'd caught sight of her near Piccadilly last Friday.'

'And she fell for it?'

'Not only that, but then we had the most stunning coincidence of all. I hadn't specified any time, naturally, but she asked me if it had been just before lunch; so, of course, I agreed, and then it all came out.'

'All what?'

'The reason for her being in London, you oaf. She was on her way to lunch with guess who? Think that one over while I get us another drink.'

'My turn,' I said, automatically rising and gathering up the empty glasses.

'There could only be one answer to account for this hubble bubble,' I told her, a few minutes later, 'and therefore I guess that her assignation was with Julian.'

'Correct. Interesting, don't you think?'

'It must have been rather a hasty lunch, though, since he had to get back to his office, to be murdered by two o'clock.'

'She claims he never turned up.'

'Oh, I see. Whereupon, she nipped over to Thurgoods and stabbed him in a fit of pique?'

'That's not her version. She said she'd written to him, saying she would be in London and suggesting he might give her lunch, as there was something she wanted to explain. I've no idea what it was, but she told me she had suggested the Savoy at one-thirty, because she knew he often lunched there, and it was a place where she could hang around for a bit if he were late or failed to show up.'

'She was fully prepared for that?'

'Well, she said she had purposely not given him her address; so he wouldn't have been able to let her know if he couldn't make it.'

'How long did she wait?'

'Until nearly two, so she says.'

'I should say the same in her place, but I wouldn't necessarily believe me, would you? In the circumstances, it indicates rather abnormal patience.'

'She claims to have spent ten or fifteen minutes in the grill-room side, and then, thinking he might have misunderstood her, went across to the restaurant, to look for him there. Apparently she spent a bit more time peering into the faces of all the unaccompanied males, which must have caused quite a sensation. On the other hand, she is a bit shortsighted, so it's not quite so daft as it sounds.'

'Didn't she bump into anyone she knew, on this peregrination?'

'Evidently not.'

'What about waiters? Wouldn't some of them have recognised her? After all, she was a minor celebrity, in her day.'

'In her day is right, but she's been living more or less in obscurity for years now. No, the trouble with a story like this is that it could be true down to the last detail, and it could be sheer cock and bull.'

'She hasn't told it to the police, by any chance?'

'I put that to her, as a possible course of action, but she wasn't keen. She pointed out that, since Julian never arrived, she had nothing to the purpose to tell them. She did say she'd be ready to tell everything about her movements if it became necessary, but she was hoping to keep out of it. She's just opened this hotel and the last thing she wants is the kind of publicity that would come from being associated, however innocently, with a sensational murder case.'

'That's logical; but, my word, she's got an answer for everything, this Jasmine, hasn't she?'

Lighting a fresh cigarette, Betty said thoughtfully: 'That remains to be seen. There are still a few questions that haven't been asked yet, and that's what we're on our way for.'

'Does she know what's in store?'

'Perhaps she does. Incidentally, I'm afraid I threw you to the lions, there, Tessa. I pretended I had arranged to drive you to Stratford for an audition, and, as you'd probably be kept hanging about for hours, it might suit us to stay the night.'

'Thanks very much,' I said bitterly. 'So I am not even a chaperone, or a map reader. I'm just an excuse; and a pretty flimsy one, at that, I might add. Stars of my calibre are not kept hanging about for hours.'

'Oh well, you couldn't expect someone like Jasmine

to know that. I don't suppose she's even heard of you.'

I glanced up, in some alarm. There was nothing in Betty's remark to warrant it, for I was accustomed to her light-hearted disparagements. It was the demeanour of the three red-faced gentlemen which had caused misgivings. Their eyes still bulged with the same thrill of excitement, but their voices were stilled. It was all too plain that every ounce of their attention was now fastened on the conversation of the two females at the next table.

Fifteen

Betty's relatively placid mood prevailed for the rest of the journey, and her driving moderated accordingly. She was one of those people whose poise and judgement were actively improved by a couple of stiff gins, and should really have been compelled to undergo a breathalyser test in reverse to ensure that the alcohol content was adequate for the safety and comfort of her passengers.

We bowled along at a sober seventy miles per hour, and, once or twice, I even ventured to drag my eyes from the road to let them range over the countryside or peer down at the map.

'Toby's house is not far from here,' I remarked, as we sailed through Stokenchurch. 'If I'd known it was so near, I'd have suggested stopping off for lunch. We might do that, on our way home tomorrow.'

'Depends if we stay until tomorrow.'

'And that, I take it, depends on our reception. You don't propose to risk a lacing of arsenic in the soup?'

'Shouldn't think there's much danger of that. I doubt if she's the type to commit murder. Hasn't the guts, for one thing. What bothers me is that I doubt if she's even capable of running an hotel efficiently. It doesn't seem quite in her line somehow. She's the type who should have married and had half a dozen children in the Cotswolds.'

'I wonder why she didn't?'

'Oh, she was all set for it. Got engaged five minutes

after leaving school, but nothing came of it. It was rather a squalid business. The young man was reputed to have thrown her over when her family lost all their money. She was probably well out of it because he got into a bad scrape himself, soon afterwards; but perhaps she's stayed faithful to his memory. However, that's neither here nor there. What I feel about Jasmine is that she knows a lot more than she's told, and I have a purely private reason for wishing to know what it is.'

'So you have,' I agreed. 'I keep forgetting.'

We lunched at Banbury and, two miles out of Shipston-on-Stour, came upon a discreet signboard with the words: Forest of Arden Hotel. Turn Left One Hundred Yards; which Betty proceeded to do.

'Oh God, is that what it's called? No wonder you were so cagey.'

However, after this ominous introduction, the exterior of the hotel was reassuring. It was a medium-sized, two-storey building, neither aggressively Elizabethan, nor festooned with all the painted tubs, wheelbarrows and hanging baskets which so often presage a rough passage through the frozen peas and scampi, in the dining-room.

The decor, in short, was right, the audience in its place; and only the players lowered the tone.

The reception desk was just inside the main door, which opened straight into a large, comfortably furnished and cheerful-looking lounge; but the only visible occupants were a forlorn and fidgety group of customers who clustered hungrily round the unattended desk.

Bypassing this sad little bunch, Betty and I headed for two armchairs, beside the open brick fireplace at the opposite end of the room.

'I think we should order tea,' she said. 'I know you're

not an addict, but it gives one a clue to the general standards. A whisky and soda tells you nothing, but tea is the acid test.'

'Also it might create some misplaced notions about our own general standards, if we asked for whisky at four in the afternoon,' I pointed out, and was answered by a raven-like croak from a nearby chair.

This had emanated from the puffy folds of an elderly and tousled lady, who was slumped down about three yards away from us. Her rumpled skirt had wriggled well above her fat knees, and she was evidently in a state of severe mental distress. She gave the impression that, about three weeks ago, someone had advised her to have a good cry, and she had been at it ever since.

'I've been telling them, and telling them, and telling them,' the croak continued, as its owner flapped one hand in a clumsy gesture, which none the less conveyed a sense of hopelessness and disgust, 'but whassergood?'

'Apparently, the licensing hours are not very strictly observed, after all,' I murmured to Betty.

She nodded gloomily and pressed a bell beside the fireplace: 'No harm in trying, I suppose?'

Meanwhile, a flicker of activity at the other end of the room had attracted my attention, and I saw that a dumpy, capable-looking woman was now in charge of the reception desk. I cannot say why I instinctively associated her with capability, unless it was for some passing resemblance to Sandy, for no one could have looked more harassed, or less competent to deal with the waiting customers, who were now petitioning her from all sides. She certainly filled none of my preconceived notions about Jasmine, and Betty did not give her a second glance.

It occurred to me to go across and consult her about

the correct procedure for ordering tea, and, at the same time, tip her off that one of the guests had been raiding the cellar, but it seemed unkind to load her with fresh burdens, and also it proved to be unnecessary. Betty's clever manoeuvre with the bell had brought results, and a prim-faced and pallid young waitress came niggling down the room towards us.

'Did you ring?' she asked somewhat incredulously.

I was all for denying it, but Betty was made of sterner stuff and admitted, with great aplomb, that we wished to order tea.

Without replying, the waitress glanced over her shoulder. There could be no doubt that her intention was to verify the time, by the clock over the reception desk, in order to tell us that we were either too late, or too early for tea, but the operation was not completed for, in the course of it, she caught sight of the Croaker.

Simultaneously, the Croaker caught sight of the waitress, and, surprisingly enough, some ripples of animation fought their way to the surface.

'Ah, Brenda,' she croaked, with heavy archness. 'Still flying about, are you? You fly here, and you fly here, and you fly here. Brenda and I are old friends,' she explained, turning to us and nodding impressively. 'We have some great old times together, don't we, Brenda? And how's that naughty young man of yours? Shushush! Not a word! Shan't say a word!'

'Come on, upsy daisy, now, and I'll help you to your room,' Brenda said, in a voice of loathing. The Croaker had caught hold of her arm and she was wriggling about in a fury of embarrassment.

'No, thank you, Brenda, dear. Quite comferble here ... just leave the old girl alone. You got enough to do without ... You fly about ... you.'

'We have ordered some tea,' Betty said loudly. 'Won't you join us?'

Knocked off her precarious balance by the brusque interruption, the Croaker slackened her grip, and, releasing herself with a deft and practised movement, Brenda darted away. Obviously, it was not the first encounter of its kind, and perhaps it was her method of extricating herself which had earned her the reputation of being such a flyer.

I watched her as she skirted the desk whence the clamorous customers had now departed, although not, as I had been sorry to notice, to whatever bedrooms had been allotted to them, but out through the main door, with bag and baggage, and into a waiting Mini bus. Meanwhile, the Croaker having instantly relapsed into inertia, Betty grimaced at me and muttered: 'What a fiasco! Good thing we left our cases in the car.'

'We shan't prove anything by walking out, though.'

'It will prove something for me. I told Jasmine what time to expect us, and she ought to have been prepared. Since she's going to such lengths to make a success of this place, the fact that it's a perfect shambles proves that she's an incompetent ass and not the one I'm looking for.'

This verdict left me as much in the dark as ever, but I did not press for explanations because there had been yet another development at the reception desk. A tall dark woman, of about the same age as Betty, had driven her car up to the main entrance and walked rapidly into the foyer. It was quite a day for people reminding me of other people, and for a moment I mistook this one for Joannie. The receptionist's face had puckered with relief, at the sight of her, and she had discreetly nodded her head in our direction. Whereupon, the newcomer dropped her bag and gloves on the desk and hurried towards us. I was relieved to find that, in full face, she bore only the most superficial resemblance to Joannie, and her anxious, uncertain expression was altogether unlike.

Oblivious of the Croaker, who appeared to be in a coma, she approached Betty, with outstretched hands, saying: 'Oh, my dear, I'm most frantically sorry. I do hope they've been looking after you? I should have been here hours ago, literally, but guess what? A puncture, of all utterly maddening things! Wouldn't you know?'

'Oh, hallo, Jasmine,' Betty said dourly. 'It doesn't matter at all. I don't think you know Tessa?'

'No, but I'm enchanted to meet you. How do you do? I know you terribly well by sight, of course. All those fabulous films!'

I could not resist a sideways glance at Betty, but the gushing reception had done nothing to soften that proud spirit, and she only said: 'I'm afraid we can't stop, after all, Jasmine. Tessa got through this audition caper quicker than she expected, and she's dead set on getting back to London tonight.'

Reeling around in the lions' den, into which my perfidious friend had cast me, I loyally uttered no protest, and only simpered inanely, when Jasmine rounded on me in passionate entreaty:

'Oh, you can't mean it? We were all so thrilled when Betty said she was bringing you, and Chef has worked himself into a frenzy of excitement. He's a terrific fan. I telephoned from London yesterday, and laid the whole thing on. You've been put in our grandest suite, with rather a darling little sitting-room, so that you can be absolutely private, if you want to. Oh, do, please, change your mind!'

I waited for my cue from Betty, but, at this point,

the Croaker suddenly revived and dealt herself a hand in the game:

'Mustn't go,' she said fretfully. 'Everybody flying about ... Gets on my nerves ...'

This acted like a whiplash on Jasmine, who spun round with blazing eyes, demanding angrily: 'How the hell ... ?' Then, with a visible effort to control herself, she added more gently: 'Come along, Mother, it's time for your rest. Let me help you up.'

'No, no, you got valble business ... I know all about it ... Mustn't let them get away ...'

'It's quite all right; nobody's going away,' Jasmine said, pushing her hand behind the old woman's back, and hoisting her up as easily as if she had been a rag doll. The Croaker appeared to find this perfectly normal, if a trifle unsettling, and, with a final peevish flap of the hands, allowed herself to be dragged away.

I had stepped forward in case assistance were needed, but Jasmine, red in the face and with compressed lips froze me off. Then, with another gallant effort to pretend that all was well, she said: 'At any rate, I beg you not to leave until I get back. My mother is not very well, as you see, but there's nothing to worry about.'

They shuffled slowly down the room, watched, with varying degrees of trepidation, by Betty and myself at one end of it, and by the receptionist at the other. When the cortege reached the foot of the staircase, I turned to Betty, who answered my inquiring look with a resigned shrug.

'What a bore! I suppose we're stuck with it now.'

'You mean, we do spend the night?'

'Can't see how we can get out of it. Come on,' she said, gathering up her bag and dressing-case. 'Let's go and inspect these twee little rooms they've got for us.'

She signed the register first, and I wrote 'Mrs Robin Price' underneath. The receptionist swivelled the book round and peered at the result.

'Anything wrong?' I asked.

'Oh, good gracious, no, nothing at all. It's just that ... well, I see you use your married name. Quite understandable, of course. Don't want every Tom, Dick and Harry ...'

'Oh, but I do,' I said brightly, turning the book round again and writing 'Theresa Crichton', in brackets, under my first entry, 'Tom, Dick and Harry is exactly what I do want. There! How's that?'

'Oh, how very nice! And you're our first celebrity. I am sure your visit will bring us luck.'

I sneaked a look, to see how Betty was swallowing this sugary pill, but the incident appeared to have escaped her. She had been busily stowing away her scarf and other belongings in the dressing-case, which she closed with a snap, saying: 'There! Now we can carry our own cases up, if you like.'

The receptionist was appalled by the suggestion. She insisted that the hall porter would be back on duty, at any moment, and that we were not to put ourselves to any such trouble.

'It will be a far worse trouble to me to sleep in my underclothes,' Betty grumbled, as we trailed up to the first floor, 'but perhaps she intends to spring out and fetch our luggage herself as soon as we're out of sight.'

It was a wide, shallow staircase, carpeted with the best red Wilton, and the landing above exuded the same atmosphere of unostentatious comfort. Except for the tiny gilt number on each of its white-painted doors, it could have been part of a well-cared-for private house, and our apartments were equally attractive.

They faced over the garden and were fitted out in the same style as all the rest.

'Must have cost a packet,' I remarked, as we did the tour.

'A very pretty penny, I should say. Oh, soap and towels, too. Well, at least we can wash our hands while we're waiting. Let's see if the hot water is hot.'

She turned on the tap and I strolled into my own little bathroom, and followed suit. Then, having nothing else to occupy me, I wandered back towards Betty's room again.

I was halfway across the sitting-room, which separated our two bedrooms, when I stopped in my tracks and more or less turned into a pillar of salt. The open door gave me a full length view of Betty, and I could follow every move in her peculiar game. She was standing beside the bed and deliberately shaking out the contents of a black, patent-leather bag. As I watched, she turned it right side up again and ran her hand round the lining. Then, slowly and meticulously, she picked up each object off the bed, examining it carefully, before replacing it in the bag.

I retreated a few steps towards the window, until she was out of sight, then collapsed, in a palpitating heap, into an armchair, all my scrupulously repressed fears surging up to the surface again. However firmly my charitable nature might proclaim that rifling someone else's bag did not prove intent to blackmail, common sense loudly replied that this was precisely the kind of activity that a blackmailer would engage in. Furthermore, there was no getting round the fact that Betty's own crocodile bag was reposing on the table beside me; whereas the black patent one was the very same that Jasmine had left on the reception desk, when she first came over to greet us.

(ii)

In fact, it was Jasmine, herself, who dragged our luggage upstairs, and she was followed into the room by the sullen Brenda, bearing a tray of tea. Betty fell upon this, with whoops of joy, but I said pettishly that I did not feel like tea any more. It was really a shameful performance. There I should have been, pointing the finger of scorn and denouncing Betty from the rooftops, and there I actually was, tossing my head and proudly refusing a cup of tea.

'Have some yourself, then?' this Judas said to Jasmine.

'Thanks. I'm dying for a cup, after that fearsome journey.'

'Oh, by the way,' Betty said, in an unconvincingly penitent tone, 'I have a confession to make. I seem to have picked up someone else's bag, by mistake.'

She disappeared into her bedroom, and I could only be grateful that she had not, so far, thrown the blame for this little oversight on to me. She emerged, carrying the bag, and saying, with a light laugh: 'I do hope the owner isn't having the vapours?'

'Perfectly all right, my dear,' Jasmine said calmly. 'It's mine, as it happens. Didn't even know I'd lost it,' she added, opening the bag and glancing indifferently at the contents. 'Fantastic what rubbish one collects, during a few days in London, isn't it? All sorts of dates and numbers scribbled on bits of paper, and one hasn't the faintest idea what they mean. One writes them down in a haze of alcohol, knowing quite well they'll lie about for weeks, and then get chucked in the wastepaper basket.'

I found myself warming to her, for it was precisely the kind of thing that was always happening to me.

Moreover, the evidence had shown her to be as much sinned against as sinning, and anyone who was saddled with the Croaker had my heartfelt sympathy.

'Mother's in bed now,' Jasmine announced, as though reading my thoughts. 'I am sorry you came in for that fracas downstairs. It wouldn't have happened if one had been here oneself, instead of parked on the roadside with a bloody flat tyre. Dorothy, my partner, can cope marvellously with the routine things; she's worked in the hotel business for centuries; but she goes into a flat spin when Mother has one of these jags. Anyway, I'm madly grateful to you both for staying.'

'Does she often get like this?' Betty asked.

'Not nowadays, thank God. I've got things fairly well under control, but I gather she wandered off on her own, some time this morning, and came back absolutely sozzled, as you saw. It wouldn't have mattered so much, only unfortunately they were so busy searching for her in all the wrong places that not one of them noticed that she'd more or less passed out in full view of the guests. Apparently, she completely scared off one little party, who'd booked in for three days.'

I mumbled something fatuous about there being plenty more something or other, but Betty cut this cackle by saying: 'How long has it been going on?'

'Oh, for years,' Jasmine replied wearily. 'And the sad part is, she's the sweetest person imaginable, when she's in her right mind. She used to be so gay and pretty, too, if you can believe such a thing.'

'What about a cure?'

'My dear, we've tried every one in the book; some of them have worked, too, though only for a time. Six months is about the longest she's managed to stay sober. I don't believe there is any permanent cure, unless the patient sincerely wants it, and my poor Mama doesn't. Why should she?'

'I don't know,' Betty said. 'Why shouldn't she?'

'It's gone on too long, for one thing; ever since my father died.'

'Was it the reason for leaving London?'

'Partly. It was much harder to keep tabs on her there, when one was working; but, apart from that, we'd both talked about moving, for ages. London's a rotten place, if you're hard up.'

'All the same, it was rather sudden, wasn't it?' Betty asked. She made no apology for this inquisition, and, curiously enough, Jasmine gave no sign of resenting it.

'Very sudden,' she agreed, 'but a couple of things brought it to a head. At least, one of them did, and the other made it possible.'

'It's the second which interests me. I refer, of course, to the fact that you could afford to.'

'I am going to explain that. I'd already made up my mind to.'

I wondered why this should be, and Jasmine obligingly clarified the point for me:

'I'd been planning to tell you about it, because I have an idea you may be up against the same sort of thing which blighted my own life, and it wouldn't be fair to hold back anything which could conceivably help you.'

For a while, it seemed that, with this cryptic statement, Jasmine had performed a neat job of table turning. With one twist, she had thrown Betty on the defensive. I recognised all the signs in the fussy way in which she picked up the crocodile bag and scrabbled inside it for cigarettes and lighter. Both of them seemed to have forgotten my existence, which was not very flattering, but I bore it cheerfully as the lesser of two evils.

'You see, Betty, one wouldn't have a dog's chance of making you understand why one accepted the money to buy this place, when it was offered, unless you knew all the circumstances.'

'Offered, did you say?'

'Yes, but that comes later. It all began about fifteen years ago. I expect you knew my father committed suicide?'

'No one of my generation could help knowing it.'

'Yes, it did make quite a stir,' Jasmine said bitterly. 'Not such a sensation as Julian's murder, perhaps, but that was only because the full story never came out. All most people knew was that good old, upstanding General Hawkes had put a bullet through his head, while taking a stroll in the woods. Don't worry, I won't harrow you with the details. My father was weak and vain, and he got himself into a squalid situation, which he was too cowardly to have brought into the open. I've got over that years ago. What I still can't forgive is that, with that situation and his total inability to face up to it, he didn't kill himself at the start; that he had to go crawling on, year after year, feebly hoping for a miracle to rescue him, until there was nothing left except mortgages and debts.'

'Until the blackmailer had bled him dry, to coin a phrase?'

'It's the right one, you know. And the stupidest, most wasteful part of all was that my mother would have stood by him, if he'd told her the truth. She'd have been deeply shocked, and all that, but she was mad about him, and she'd have been a rock, whatever vices or crimes he'd been guilty of. As it was, she had to endure all the shock and horror, just the same, and most of the pittance they managed to save from the wreck has been frittered away on these useless cures. The rest, one need hardly add, has gone on the bottle.'

'Tough luck,' Betty said laconically. 'I didn't know.'

'No one did, apart from the immediate family, and the blackmailer, of course, and he was never caught. At least, that's what I always believed. Then, out of the blue, I discovered that, all these years, there has been one other person who knew all about it. Two guesses who that was!'

'Didn't it strike you that he might have been the blackmailer himself?'

'No. Mind you, I think he was every sort of four-letter word, and, although I didn't kill him, I'm eternally grateful to whoever did. A risky thing to say, maybe, but it's true.'

'Yet you still didn't consider him capable of blackmail?'

'The point is that Julian wasn't out for money. He'd got stacks of his own, for one thing. What he was after was kicks, and he got them by digging away, like some ghastly, perverted mole, unearthing all the discreditable facts about people who were supposed to be his friends. It was a pretty revolting hobby, but at least he practised it in private, and didn't do any active harm; until recently, that is.'

'You mean, when he decided to publish and be damned?'

'Oh, I don't think he ever meant that seriously, do you? For a start, it really would have damned him; particularly in the eyes of the people he was most anxious to ingratiate himself with, the people who were so grand and impregnable that even he was powerless to dig up any dirt about them. No, I've been mulling it over, and I've come to the conclusion that the publishing yarn was just a tease, an extra threat to hold over his victims' heads. What he really wanted was to fish them up, one by one, and watch them squirm. So far as I know, he began with me, though one can't say for sure about that. At any rate, my reactions must have given him a terrific boost. I squirmed good and proper, I might tell you.'

'Incidentally, I wonder how he got hold of all his shoddy information? It can't have been all that easy.'

'Oh, by the most foul means you can think of; bribing servants, chatting up the tradesmen, all that kind of thing. He cultivated dozens of weird people, you know, who were quite outside his class. I used to believe it was because they were the kind he could condescend to, but one sees now that he had a much more sinister motive. I think Barnes may have had a bit to do with it, too. He's so damned pompous and respectable these days, it gives one a pain, but I gather he's been on to a few sharp practices, in his day. Curiously enough, he began life as a private in my father's regiment, but that's sheer coincidence. He'd left the Army long before the time we're talking about. Anyway, the point is that Julian wasn't a bit squeamish about revealing his sources; quite proud of it, in fact. He actually confessed to me, with great glee, that he'd become very chummy with my ex-governess, after my father died. A terribly dim female, so far as one remembers. They can't have had much in common, but presumably she listened at a few keyholes, in her time. She'd got her facts right, too. I could hardly believe my eyes, when I read it all in Julian's diary, while he calmly requested me to type it out for him. I lost my head and told him what he could do with it.'

'And what was his reaction to that?'

'Oh, he was enchanted. He'd got right under my skin just as he'd hoped. I thought he'd die laughing. I could easily have throttled him, myself, then, but I didn't. Thank God, I had enough wits to chuck it in. And it wasn't only my own feelings which were scarified, I might tell you. He'd written things about someone I used to ... know rather well. He turned out to be a bit of a heel, actually, but the point was that he regarded Julian as a true friend. He probably does, to this day, and I hope to God he never finds out what the dear friend really felt about him, and how he revelled in his downfall.'

Jasmine's long exposition had given Betty ample time to regain her self-possession, and she now returned to the pitiless probing.

'You say you just chucked it in, and refused to have any more to do with Julian, or his diaries, but it isn't quite true, is it? You had asked him to meet you for lunch, last Friday?'

Still unresentful, Jasmine said frankly: 'I know it was a cowardly thing to do. I suppose one has an unlucky heritage where moral fibre is concerned, but, when I'd had time to simmer down and see things clearly, I got in a complete funk. I realised it wouldn't take long for him to trace me; and I also knew how vindictive he was. I'd really made myself even more vulnerable by walking out on him, and I wanted to wipe out that impression and somehow convince him that this hotel wasn't a desperately serious enterprise, just something I'd taken on to help Dorothy get started. I daresay he wouldn't have swallowed it, but it was the best protection I could think of.'

'Well, thanks for telling me,' Betty said. 'It hasn't helped much, but I appreciate it all the same. And you needn't worry; I shan't breathe a word. As for my little mouse-like friend over there, you're quite safe. You'd be surprised to learn what secrets lurk behind those baby blue eyes.'

I should have been equally surprised to learn it myself, but Jasmine nodded her head, as though she understood perfectly.

'You may as well hear it all,' she said. 'As I recall, you were chiefly interested in how I got the money.'

Betty ground out her cigarette and stared back appraisingly: 'So I was, Jasmine, but that was some time ago, and I believe everything you've told me. Obviously, the rest of the story is irrelevant.'

'Thank you for saying that. As a matter of fact, it was Lavender who made the thing possible. Mrs Teddy, to you.'

'You don't say? Well, that certainly is a turn up for the book! I would never have credited her with largesse on that scale.'

'It was a loan; interest free, and repayable over ten years.'

'Even so ...'

'Oh, I agree. Fantastically generous terms, but poor old Lavender has always been rather a good friend. I was civil to her in the days when I had no axes to grind, when Julian and his pa were furious about Teddy marrying her, and Julian, in particular, was unbelievably spiteful. She and I had some feeble joke going about our both having flower names, and I used to meet her occasionally even when I'd lost touch with the rest of the family.'

'Congratulations,' Betty said dryly. 'It was a hell of a lot of bread to come floating back on the waters.'

Jasmine looked down, pleating the hem of her skirt with her fingers, as she spoke.

'Well, one would be an ass to resurrect the doubts,

after baring one's soul, so to speak, so here goes: of course, Lavender had an ulterior motive, too.'

'Ah!'

'As I say, we'd kept in touch, and she knew how dead set I was on getting Mother out of London. When she found I was transcribing Julian's diary, she offered me a deal. She really wanted me to destroy the manuscript, but I told her it was out of the question. I couldn't see how it was to be done, for one thing, with Julian guarding it like the Minotaur, and I simply wouldn't have had the nerve. So we compromised. I was to keep her informed of every detail that he'd written, and, wherever possible, to leave out, or tone down references to herself. She's got a fantastic chip on her shoulder about her humble origins.'

'I believe you.'

'Anyway, I agreed to co-operate, although, of course, I had to back out almost at once. You know all about that. I offered to return the money, but she wouldn't take it. She's a good sort, in her way, and she said that my throwing in the sponge might be the best thing that could happen. It could be ages before Julian was able to replace me, and she'd meanwhile got another plan for putting a spanner in his works.'

'What plan?'

'She didn't say, and I didn't ask. I couldn't wait to push the whole bloody business out of my mind.'

'Well, I suppose we'll never know now,' Betty said. 'And perhaps it has no importance. Time for a drink, I should say. How about you, Tessa?'

'I'll fetch them,' Jasmine said, standing up. 'We're still a bit short-handed, for the moment. What's it to be?'

'Just one other question, before I tell you. This one, admittedly, is sheer, straightforward curiosity, but I've been wondering what made you hint that you and I might be in the same boat?'

'Oh well,' Jasmine said awkwardly, fiddling with the door knob, 'forgive me, but I passed five of my formative years with a man who was being blackmailed, literally to death. It doesn't take me long to recognise the symptoms.'

One by one, during their dialogue, some little mental pennies had been dropping into place. With Jasmine's *coup de grâce*, the last handful clattered into their slots, and the true explanation for Betty's weird behaviour was at last revealed. Not a blackmailer, but the victim of one; not Peter Hitchen's persecutor, but his fellow-sufferer; and not A, or B, but Robin's Mrs X, in the flesh.

I had rarely felt more shattered in my life, and, had it not been for the awful example of the Croaker, should have called for a treble brandy on the spot.

Sixteen

Dinner at the Forest of Arden had fully justified Jasmine's build up, and, afterwards, Betty and I had sat in our dinky sitting-room, talking far into the night. The result was that on Tuesday morning normal habits proved stronger than good resolutions, and I overslept.

I was rather flustered to awake and see ten minutes to eleven on my travelling clock, for Betty was a great bustler about in the early hours, and I sauntered into her bedroom, bracing myself for some harsh words about my sloppy habits, etcetera. To my relief, it was empty, and a furtive peep from the bathroom window showed that her car had gone from the Residents' parking space. I concluded that she had given me up as a bad job and swept off to London, on her own.

However, when I emerged from the bathroom, about forty minutes later, she was back in her room. She haughtily informed me that she had been for an early morning hike, and had also had the forethought to take the car into Shipston, to fill up with petrol and all the rest of it in readiness for the return journey. My feeble pleas that we might stay for lunch, and give the Chef another tonic to the spirits, were brushed aside on the grounds that we had achieved what she came for and must therefore push on. She added that, since the staff was so thin on the ground as to be almost invisible, I could begin by carrying my own case down to the car.

I rang Toby's house, to ask if we should be welcome

there, but the gardener's wife told me that he had gone to London, on business. She added that she fancied he had half a mind to spend the night there; so then I had to try and get hold of Sebastian, with instructions about the spare room, lest that half should prove the stronger. But, although I rang three times, at ten minute intervals, there was no reply from Beacon Square, indicating that he had slipped out for a somewhat protracted toddle. One way and another, I set out for London in a grisly mood.

I pulled myself out of it, by degrees, and, when we were nearly home, ventured to introduce a topic which had not yet been thrashed out.

'When you paid me that undeserved compliment about my discretion, etcetera, Betty, I couldn't understand what you were driving at; but you must have believed that I knew all along about your being blackmailed?'

'You mean, Robin didn't tell you?'

'He told me he was up to his neck in a case, but no names, and what Sandy calls no pack drill.'

'Well, good for him! I thought he was rather decent, even before I knew he was your beloved.'

'I can't think why that took you so long.'

'Dim of me, wasn't it? It was the same kind of mental block that occurs when you meet the grocer in church. You chat him up across the counter, every morning, and then you absolutely can't place this well-dressed creature, leering at you as you walk up the aisle.'

'I don't ever remember seeing grocers leering at me in church,' I said, pondering this phenomenon. 'I must remember to be on my guard.'

'In Robin's case, it wasn't a perfect parallel, because I knew you'd married a policeman, but it happened when I was on the other side of the world. When I thought of him at all, I visualised some beefy personage under a helmet, asking everyone what seems to be the trouble. I certainly never associated him with that suave type I'd been meeting at Scotland Yard.'

'And that's why you beat it, like a bat out of hell, when you saw him at our party?'

'Yes, I'm not easily fazed, as you know, but I lost my head that time. It came to me that you must know all about this little trouble of mine, and it was a nasty old shock.'

'But I didn't know a thing.'

'So you've now told me. Pity I let the cat out, wasn't it? Still no harm done, I daresay.'

'I don't even know how the case is progressing. Julian's murder has shoved everything else into the background. Have there been any developments?'

'Not that I know of. I had been hoping to precipitate a few. Had my eye on Jasmine, in fact. I know she's long since dropped out of most circles, but doubtless she still has friends in various camps; and I've always had a hunch there's a woman's hand in this. Splashing out into the hotel trade, when she was supposed to be broke, was rather a timely coincidence. However, that was a false trail, and, personally, I'm back at the beginning again.'

'I suppose you are, but, even if she's in the clear, on the blackmail score, it seems to me that she's right back on the murder suspect list. After all, it turns out that she had a much stronger motive than either of us guessed, and we've agreed that her story about fooling around for a whole hour at the Savoy could have been pure invention.'

'It could equally well have been true. She had made it impossible for Julian to let her know, if he couldn't keep the appointment.'

'But had she really, Betty? I was thinking it over, afterwards, and it struck me that all that part was a bit implausible. Admittedly, he didn't know her address, but he did know that she intended to arrive at the Savoy at one-thirty. If he couldn't meet her there, all he had to do was telephone the desk, and leave a message for her. He was terribly well known there, and they'd have fallen over backwards to do anything he wanted; and, if you ask me, that's actually what he would have done.'

'Well, maybe he did, but, with the silly creature meandering about all over the place, it's quite easy to see how the message never got delivered. No, kiddo, you'll have to dream up something stronger than that to make a case against her.'

'And don't imagine I haven't.'

'Oh, really? Let's hear it, then.'

'How about this? Let's say that, when she wrote suggesting a meeting, she never mentioned the Savoy at all. How about if she said she'd go to his office at one-thirty, instead?'

'Funny time to choose, knowing his social routine.'

'Yes, but the best of all, from her point of view; and she could have gambled on curiosity making him sacrifice the social scene, for once. Don't you see, Betty? Assuming that she'd been handed out one of those private lift keys, when she was working for Julian, and had stalked off without returning it, can't you see how easily it would have been managed? All she had to do was lurk about, until she saw Julian go in and Barnes come out, and Hey Presto! Up she goes, knowing she's got a clear hour and a half to persuade him to hand over the diaries, or else. Doesn't that make sense?'

I had become quite enamoured of the theory, as I went along, but Betty knocked it into the ground.

'It's a loony idea,' she said scornfully. 'She'd have known perfectly well that there wasn't a hope in hell of his giving up the diaries, and I've told you already that she hasn't the guts to commit murder.'

'Doesn't blackmail require guts, of a kind?'

'I wouldn't have said so. Wits, perhaps, but not guts. It's a sneaky, cowardly sort of crime, with the minimum of personal risk to the perpetrator. And this fellow, whoever he may be, is as sneaky as they come.'

'But still, you've had no more demands?'

'Not a murmur, though how long this'll last is anyone's guess. I find it a trifle unnerving, this constant feeling that he may be someone I come face to face with every day.'

'What I can't understand is why you didn't go to the police, in the first place. I mean, you can't have had anything so very dreadful on your conscience, and, even if it had all come out, your friends would have rallied.'

'Easy to say, my little simpleton, and I might even have done it, if it had been just my own guilty secret. Unfortunately, a special sort of courage is needed, to gamble on landing another person in gaol for the rest of his life. And that's just for a starter. He's only one of the people who stood to get caught.'

'Tricky,' I admitted.

'Very,' she replied, pulling up outside our next door neighbour's house. It was as near as she could get to our front door, because Toby's Mercedes filled the space in front of it.

'Will you come in, and say Hello to him?' I asked.

'Not today, thanks. I feel hot, and dusty, and discouraged.'

She looked it, too; all the bounce and bossiness drained out of her, and all bolts shot. She reminded me a little of Sandy, after a blistering session with Bobs, and I was prompted to say: 'Cheer up, Betty. I feel the benign fluences very strongly, at this moment, and my voices tell me that the end is not far off.'

'That's my brave little optimist,' she said, taking a cursory glance in the wing mirror, before shooting out into the traffic.

(ii)

There was no need to search for my latch key, because the front door was ajar, indicating that Sebastian's current slipping out mission had been of such urgency that he had not even bothered to take his keys. Possibly he regarded Toby's presence as sufficient safeguard against intruders, but I resolved to utter a sharp word on the subject. Had it not been for the refreshing effects of the Warwickshire air, and the even more refreshing knowledge that Betty was now *sans reproche*, if not *peur*, even sterner measures might have suggested themselves, for I trembled to think of the uproar that would have ensued had Robin arrived home ahead of me.

Even my tolerance was inadequate to withstand the next shock, which came from the gradual realisation that the house was, in fact, deserted.

I called Toby's name, as I entered the hall, then looked in the empty drawing-room. Still shouting, I galloped upstairs and thumped on the spare-room door. There was no answer and the interior was neat and anonymous.

Sebastian's room was empty, too, although neat and anonymous were hardly the words it brought to mind. I had only rarely braced myself to take a peep inside, for I knew him to be incurably untidy, which is distressing enough in itself, and I had no desire at all to pry into his private belongings.

On this occasion, anxiety overruled such niceties, and I opened the door without pausing to think. It was a disastrous move, for the scene which confronted me was so chaotic that the metaphor of the bull in the china shop came nowhere near describing it. A stranger to the house would have assumed without question that Sebastian shared his room with a rogue elephant.

Consumed with rage and self pity, I descended to my own room, where I sat down and tearfully contemplated my hard lot, which allowed me a brief and innocent jaunt to the country, only at the price of utter turmoil on my return.

As if this were not enough, I soon became aware that physical pangs were adding themselves to these bitter reflections, and I realised that I was ravenously hungry. This is a condition to which I am often prone in times of severe mental frustration. I understand it is a perfectly normal Freudian reaction, but there were complicating factors on this occasion. Betty had been in such a tearing hurry to get back to London that she had refused to stop on the way for lunch.

The kitchen was as silent as all the rest of the house, but just a little less deserted. Sebastian was seated, with his back to the door, sprawled drunkenly forward over the scrubbed deal table.

Two facts penetrated my dazed wits, before horror and revulsion took over. The first was that the bone handle of the carving knife had somehow become attached to his back; the second, that the huge dark red stain, which had seeped out over the table, was already perfectly dry.

(iii)

I was still rooted in the doorway, rigid as Lot's wife, when my already screaming nerves received a fresh assault from the front doorbell, which shrilled out just above my head. The shock of it jerked me out of my paralysis, and I stumbled into the hall and dived for the door handle, gasping and whimpering as I tugged at it, for I was only a fraction more terrified of remaining alone in the house than of the possibility of sharing it with a murderer.

Confronting me on the doorstep was my cousin Toby. He had every excuse for being taken aback by his reception, for he had his nasty old hat pulled down over his eyes, creating a most sinister effect, and I reeled backwards with a rending scream. When it sank in that it was he and not the murderer, I reeled forward again, still screaming, and collapsed on top of him.

Paradoxically, however, Toby was about the most useful member of the public that Fate could have sent me, in that crisis. Mortality loomed so large in his fears that a cold in the nose was enough to cast him into the jitters; the mention of death, let alone a violent and unnatural one, practically brought on the palsy.

Once I had screamed the initial shock out of my system, I was so busy trying to calm him down that I succeeded, even more effectively, in calming myself in the process. In the space of ten minutes, I had telephoned Robin, closed the kitchen door on the dreadful sight within, poured us a stiff brandy apiece, and got Toby launched on an account of his movements, since arriving in London.

'Mrs Parkes told me you'd already left,' I said. 'So you must have got here before lunch.'

'Is this habit infectious?' he asked crossly. 'You are hectoring me like a police detective.'

'It's for your own good, my boy. A real detective will be taking over from me any time now, so we'd better put you through your paces. If there are any tiresome little gaps in your story, we may as well fit them in with something that at least sounds authentic.'

'Quite unnecessary. I didn't kill whatsisname, and I have nothing whatever to hide.'

'Glad to hear it, but the fact remains that your car was parked outside, so you must have been here at some point, and you have several hours to account for. They'll want to know about that, for a start.'

'I arrived about twelve. There was no one at home. There hardly ever is, so far as I can make out. You weren't expecting me, so there was no telling when you'd be back. I took a taxi up to the Caprice. After lunch I came back here, and I wish to God I hadn't.'

'Was the front door properly shut, or not? The first time, I mean.'

'I suppose so. I didn't notice that it wasn't.'

'Well, you'll have to be a bit more positive than that.'

He thought this over for a while, and then said that, on the whole, he inclined to the view that the door had been firmly shut. I agreed that it was a sensible view and urged him to stick to it.

'See anyone at the Caprice who recognised you?'

'No idea,' he said gloomily. 'I saw one or two that I recognised, which was enough. I asked for a corner table, in the pitch dark.'

'That's the trouble with being a misogynist. No man is an island,' I reminded him.

He had barely begun his comments on this observation, when we were interrupted by noises off. A door banged and Robin's voice called out that it was only him. Then we heard him speaking again and other voices answering. Soon afterwards, he joined us and the questioning recommenced, only, this time, I was included in it.

Toby reeled off his story very nicely and had the advantage of me, in having had a previous run-through. I stumbled a little over mine, but a straightforward account might have indicated a sang abnormally froid, and I decided to keep the fluffs and stutters in, when it came to the real performance.

When I had finished, I reverted to the subject of Sebastian's room, saying: 'I see now that it wasn't just ordinary untidiness. Someone had searched it, and they must have been in a wild hurry, too.'

Robin left us and went bounding upstairs. When he returned, he said: 'I've locked it and taken the key. It'll have to be gone over for prints. You didn't touch anything, I hope?'

'Oh, no, no, certainly not. Only the door knob, that is.'

'And nothing ... in the kitchen, either?'

'Good God, no Robin. What do you think?'

'You might have, you know ... wanted to make sure he was dead?'

'I knew he was dead. My instinct told me. Wasn't he?' I added, on a rising note.

'Yes, he was; hours before, so don't worry. They put it between eight and eleven this morning. I didn't leave until eight-thirty, so that narrows it down still more. And it doesn't look as though either of you has much to contribute. The Inspector in charge will want your statements, and, after that, we can go.'

'Go?' I repeated. 'Go where?'

'Oh, didn't I tell you? I've booked rooms for us at an hotel. We can't possibly stay here.'

'But I have to stay here, Robin.'

'Darling, what are you talking about? Believe me, it would be quite intolerable for you.'

'I'm serious, though. I dare not leave. If I were to walk out now, I know I could never return. I'm like a jockey, after a fall. The only way to get my nerve back is to climb into the saddle again. Besides, Sandy will be here tomorrow. She'll arrive at nine, and how could I let her walk in and find everything, you know ... ?'

'Poor old thing,' he said kindly. 'You're still a bit woozy, and no wonder! But, you know, we can easily get in touch with Sandy and tell her not to come. I've every intention of taking the day off tomorrow, so you won't be alone.'

'No,' I said obstinately. 'That's no good at all. What would you and I do, mooning at each other in an hotel all day? We could keep going to the cinema, I suppose, but you'd be bored silly by the evening. Anyway, I'd rather Sandy came. There'll be dozens of beastly jobs to cope with, like fending off the press, and so on, which she can take off our hands.'

'Okay, if that's what you really want?'

'Oh, it is, it absolutely is. Sandy is so marvellously bracing and unimaginative, you see. It will be such a tonic.'

'Whatever you say,' agreed this paragon among men, and I listened as he dialled the Ealing number, gave Sandy an outline of events, and responded patiently to all the roars and squawks from the other end.

To show my gratitude I offered a compromise. We should both spend the night at the hotel, on condition that he escorted me back to Beacon Square at daybreak on the morrow.

He consented to this, too, and by six o'clock I was installed in our vast, impersonal, temporary lodgings beside Victoria Station, where Robin joined me an hour or two later. Surprisingly enough, Toby had elected to come, too, and had booked himself into the room next to ours.

'What are you doing in London, anyway?' I inquired. 'I quite forgot to ask you.'

Considering his loathing of all cities, and of London in particular, it was a natural question, and he said airily: 'It's that bloody tax business again. A giant snag has come up and I thought old Fairy Montagu Dashwood might be able to wave her wand. Wednesday is her day, isn't it?'

'Very true,' I agreed. 'It is.'

I was thinking that an odd characteristic of Toby's was that, although unable to carry a name in his head for two consecutive minutes, his memory for details was excellent when it suited him.

Seventeen

Sebastian's death had temporarily wiped out other considerations, but, lying awake in our alien, twin-bedded room, I asked Robin if he did not agree that the same hand had committed both murders.

He admitted it, with reservations, although few enough to give me courage to say: 'What beats me, now that I know the truth about Betty, is why you didn't arrest her on the spot. I mean, her being there to discover the body, with a possible motive tucked away in the diaries, what stopped you?'

'You must remember that we knew nothing about the diaries then. No one had even mentioned them. That was your little contribution, and it came rather late in the day.'

'It might not have come at all, if I had known that Betty was Mrs X. Didn't it seem to you that, in my innocence, I was handing you her motive on a plate? Of course, I can say this now, because you've admitted, yourself, that the two murders are connected, and Betty has a cast-iron alibi for Sebastian's, but you can hardly have foreseen that things would turn out so conveniently for her.'

'I think it was her presence on the scene, so soon after Julian's murder, which partially ruled her out. After all, she had access to Thurgoods' second floor at all times. There would have been dozens of opportunities, without calling attention to herself so blatantly. We could find nothing to connect her with the crime, except opportunity, which is hardly enough to convict anyone.'

'Specially as dozens of other people had an equally good opportunity.'

'Isn't that one of your celebrated exaggerations? I should have said three or four, at the most.'

'Well, taking the people who had the special lift key, there's the family, for a start. And what about the secretarial staff?'

'No, not one of them, funnily enough; not even the bosses' own private secretaries. They don't seem to have trusted their employees very far. Betty was the only exception, as far as I can make out, and that was on account of being head of a department. The key and the position went together, by tradition.'

'It still leaves Barnes; and he had the best opportunity of anyone.'

'No motive, though; and a nice, tidy little alibi.'

'He really was at the pub, during the crucial period?'

'Seems like it. At any rate, he went in at about his usual time. In fact, the landlord happens to remember that it was a few minutes later than usual. He's one of those chaps you can set your watch by, apparently. Anyway, that fits with Barnes' own story about some determined hangers on in the Boardroom. He was certainly in the Pub, too, when the police went round to dig him out, about twenty minutes after the murder was discovered. Nothing to show that he was absent at any time, during the interval, although the picture there is not quite so clear.'

'Well, there you are, then!'

'No, I'm not. You've got to remember, Tessa, that all the pubs in that district are jam-packed, during the lunch hour. It would have been quite extraordinary if any particular individual's arrival or departure had been noticed. And that is particularly true of Barnes, who was such a staunch regular that he more or less formed part of the landscape.'

'Which means that it would have been rather more noticeable if he hadn't been present, than if he had.'

'Exactly. And, although they haven't found anyone to swear that he was there the whole time, neither have they found anyone to swear that he wasn't, which strikes me as more significant. It's not, by any means, a perfect alibi, but those can be double-edged, too. Innocent people rarely have perfect alibis tucked up their sleeves, ready to produce on request. The theory now is that the murderer was someone Julian brought back to the office with him. They'll go on checking and re-checking, naturally, but it doesn't appear that anyone, except for the people we've mentioned, owned that special key. And all of them are out of the race, for one reason or another.'

'I can think of at least one other who might have possessed it,' I said. 'Possibly two. I can't be certain about that, until I've done some more work on it.'

'Now, Tessa, don't you dare!'

'Don't I dare what?'

'Poke your nose in. I won't have it, do you understand? This is a dangerous, ruthless murderer we're up against. He's killed two people already, and I don't see the slightest reason why he should stop at a third. You've got to promise me to keep out of it.'

'Oh, I wasn't planning any direct action,' I assured him. 'It's just this feeling I have that the solution is all there, floating somewhere in the back of my mind, if only I could catch hold of it. All I mean to do is concentrate, until it finally breaks through. You can't object to that. I'll pass my findings on, and you can take all the necessary action, I promise you.'

'Well, if that's really all ... ?'

'It really is, Robin; and, in any case, I don't feel there's quite so much urgency about it, now that Betty's exonerated, out of the wood, and off the hook.'

Robin smiled. The room was in pitch darkness, but the smile broke out in his voice, as he said: 'And now I'd like to hear every little detail about your lovely trip to Warwickshire; and everything you talked about, on the way there and back.'

(ii)

Toby had done his utmost to persuade me to return to the country with him, but I brought out the jockey metaphor again, insisting that I must resume my life at Beacon Square immediately, or not at all, and, rather unexpectedly, Robin backed me up. He said that danger was less likely to lurk in crowded London streets than in quiet country lanes, and that he had arranged for a watch to be kept on the house. No one would be able to get in or out, without the police knowing.

Nor was this all. His passion for warning systems was insatiable, and workmen were already installing the latest device when we arrived at our front door on Wednesday morning. It was one of those two-way microphone affairs, connected to the bell, whereby I could command any caller to give his identity and credentials, before admitting him, and Robin had charged me and Toby to resort to it on all occasions.

I privately considered it to be rather a potty idea, as, until I knew who the murderer was, I did not see how any machine would help to keep him out; but Robin had such faith in it that I did not prick the bubble.

Progress had been made in other spheres, too. I had

not hitherto had occasion to appreciate the benefits of being married into the police force, for those unfortunate enough to have a murder committed on their premises. All the dismal formalities were taken out of my hands, and Sebastian's only living relatives, an uncle and aunt in Halifax, whose existence had been unknown to us, had been traced, and told of his death.

As for Sandy, her initiative and resource exceeded even my expectations. She was already installed in the little sitting-room, surrounded by piles of what she called emergency tackle, including a spirit lamp, which had been used for camping expeditions in 'days of yore'. In the course of the morning, she not only prevailed upon a removal firm to spirit away the old kitchen table but also on the local hardware shop to instal an impersonal, plastic-topped model in its place. Her crowning achievement was that, by four o'clock, she had interviewed and engaged an elderly dragon, of impeccable references, to take charge of our domestic affairs. She warned me that the salary for this desirable female would be in the region of five pounds a minute, explaining that it was no piece of cake to acquire reliable cook/housekeepers at short notice, even for the best-run establishments, and a house where the previous incumbent had been stabbed to death, in his own kitchen, hardly qualified as one of those.

'Goodness knows where we'll put her, though,' I grumbled. 'I believe Robin means to sort out Sebastian's room, as soon as he gets the official go ahead, but it will be weeks before it's habitable again.'

Sandy, of course, had everything worked out: 'Not to worry, old horse. The spare room's in apple-pie order, so we can pop her in there, for a day or two.'

In the meantime, by a blessed stroke of luck, which I would not have put it past Sandy to have engineered, a script had arrived in the morning's post, and she persuaded me to have a bash at it, pronto and *tout de suite*. I was installed on my bedroom chaise-longue, with the first of the steaming cups of coffee, which were brewed up on the spirit lamp at regular intervals throughout the morning.

I daresay she wanted me out of her hair, while she carved her imperturbable way through each little crisis that arose, and, if so, she had chosen an infallible method. It proved to be a whizz-bang of a script, too, with a part on such stuff as dreams are made, and it was only at rare moments, as the telephone rang in another part of the house, that I was reminded of poor, silly Sebastian and how much I missed him.

I turned to the last page. It contained two lines of dialogue, followed by the directions: 'Fade out.' 'End Titles.' There was a trite kind of poignancy in this, which brought all the melancholy thoughts flooding back, and, with a perversity there is no accounting for, my cherished solitude began to turn sour on me. There was nothing to fill it any longer, except a growing sense of resentment that those two working bees, Robin and Sandy, were managing so well without me, having patently reached the conclusion that the serious business of the day would proceed more smoothly with the mistress of the house safely occupied with some trivia more suited to her powers. I decided to go and make some buzzing noises of my own.

I ran into Robin on the landing. He was descending from the floor above, looking dusty and dishevelled, but annoyingly self-satisfied.

'That foul job's done at last,' he announced, following me into the little sitting-room. 'If you're ever inspired to employ a man-servant again, I would prefer an ex-Sergeant-Major, or a Trappist Monk.'

'Does either of you feel ready for a drink?' I asked. 'I imagine we'll have to do without ice.' Which just showed how limited an imagination could be. Sandy dived for some more of her camping equipment, a squat thermos flask, which she had filled with ice cubes from her own refrigerator. She then reeled off her list of the morning's achievements, which was capped by Robin's description of the sorting and packing of Sebastian's belongings, which were now in trunks, awaiting the pleasure of the couple from Halifax.

Neither of them asked me about the script, and I was too proud to mention it, as well as too fearful that they might literally pat me on the head and say what a clever girl I was.

Robin said that he would clean up and then escort us both to the hotel for lunch. He asked Sandy to reserve a table for four, because of Toby; whereupon she clapped a hand to her mouth and stared at us, in agonies of self-reproach.

'Oh, golly, chaps! What a frightful boob! He was here this morning. Popped in about eleven o'clock. There was some little bother over the income tax he wanted my advice about.'

'What a ruthless fellow he is! Did you have time to deal with it?'

'Oh yes, it was just a wee technicality. We sorted it out in a jiff, and he went off like a dog with two tails. Said he was going straight back to the country.'

'Without even saying goodbye?' I demanded petulantly.

'His own idea, old girl. He said he wouldn't disturb you, when you both had enough on your plates already.'

I recognised a slight paraphrase here, as it was not an expression which any reasonably observant person would have associated with Toby, but Robin accepted it at face value. He said cheerfully that we might just as well go round the corner to the pub, in that case.

Sandy, however, elected to stay at her post. She said she had brought the odd sandwich, and would be as right as a trivet.

'As it happens, I'm glad we're on our own,' Robin said, as we tucked into our mountains of steak and kidney pudding, which was the specialité de la maison de Plumbers Arms. 'I have something to tell you, which is for your ears alone. You remember the book carrier?'

'How could I forget it?'

'Well, it has turned up again.'

'Not really? Where?'

'Tucked away in Sebastian's bottom drawer. So there's one little mystery cleared up.'

'Do you think so? I'd say it was more mysterious than ever.'

'Well, obviously, he pinched it.'

'Why should he do that, Robin? You weren't there, but I saw his face, when we first unpacked it. There was no acquisitory gleam, I assure you. He clearly thought it was a load of old rubbish.'

'Nevertheless, he probably realised it had a market value.'

'Yes, he must have, but, I confess that you could knock me down with a feather. I never gave him a hint that it was valuable, and I'd have sworn that kind of knowledge was much too esoteric to be in his scope. Besides, for all he knew, I was intending to send it back to Thurgoods.'

'I daresay he was relying on your somewhat forgetful nature.'

'Maybe. Anyway, it hardly seems worth bothering

about now, does it? I've quite forgotten who the legal owner is, at this point.'

'No, I don't think it has any great importance. I just thought you'd be glad to hear the end of the saga.'

'Oh, I am, and I only hope it is the end. Are you going to have rhubarb and custard, or apple crumble?'

Robin, however, had become ridden with nostalgia for his office and resisted both these temptations. He said shamefacedly that he would just look in for a couple of hours, and would be back in one of Sandy's jiffies, if needed. Moreover, he insisted on first accompanying me back to the house. This was ostensibly for the purpose of warding off any armed desperadoes, who might be lurking in my path, but I think he was really dying to have a go with the new speaking box. If so, the experiment must have been disappointing. He pressed the bell twice, got no response at all, and was bracing himself for the third attempt when the door was flung open by a flustered Sandy, for all the world as though we were still living in the pre-electronic age.

She apologised profusely, saying that she had been upstairs, when the bell rang, and, in her haste to answer it, had forgotten all about the new rule.

Robin sent her back indoors, to go through the correct procedure from the beginning. This time, with all of us set and on our marks, it went off without a hitch, and he departed on his way, urging us both to take proper care in future.

Pouring some balm on Sandy's wounded self-esteem, I nerved myself to enter the kitchen so as to make some admiring noises about the new plastic table. It had certainly altered the character of the room, and when Sandy, with *amour propre* restored, had tanked off back to the grindstone, I remained there, looking about me, and assuring myself that all the ghosts had been well and truly laid.

An extra bonus arising from all this was the notion it gave me of at last being able to do something practical, in a field which had not yet been trampled over by Robin or Sandy.

Sebastian had kept most of his possessions in his own room, but one drawer in the kitchen dresser had been allocated to him, as a repository for his wristwatch, *Sunday Mirror*, box of minty toffees and sundry items of that nature. I resolved to improve the shining hour by clearing out this drawer, myself.

It was not, as it happened, a Herculean task quite in the class of the Augean Stables, for the drawer contained only a half-eaten apple, some luridly coloured postcards from European resorts, a bottle of scent called Sauvage, and an envelope containing two passport photographs. I was about to tip the whole collection into the dustbin, when, on a sentimental impulse, I paused for another glance at the photographs. They showed Sebastian's head and shoulders, in full face, and he was sporting a grey silk stock, which I well remember his having put on for the occasion. There was a black speck on it, which did not rub off, and I found that it featured in both prints. I peered at it more closely, but was finally obliged to take the photographs upstairs and study them under Robin's giant magnifying-glass, to verify my guess.

Having done so, I replaced the prints in their envelope, wrote 'Evidence?' on the outside, and pushed it into a drawer of Robin's desk. Afterwards, I remained seated for a while, pondering the implications of my latest discovery.

It was not the fact of my beloved old Indian brooch reposing now in some crooked Amsterdam jeweller's shop which chiefly bothered me. The big headache was the logical inference that Sebastian had found the key to my dressing-table drawer, where Julian's diary had been lying, for at least twenty-four hours before the brooch was removed.

Eighteen

It was the first of several developments in an eventful afternoon, and, soon after three, I had my first skirmish with the new answering technique. I performed my part with extreme nonchalance, being more than half convinced that Robin, himself, was at the front door, carrying out a spot check. When the caller, after a strange uneasy silence declared himself to be Mr Brown, I was so knocked off balance that I released the door catch before I knew what I was about.

There was no turning back, though, and I had to force myself to go into the hall and see what mischief I had performed. Instead of the expected ghost, it was the old ghost expert, Julian's father, who stood there. His face was the colour of a beetroot, and his bowler hat revolved in his nervous, pudgy fingers.

'Mrs Price? Excuse me bothering you, but could I have a word?'

His demeanour reminded me more of a stage bailiff than a murderer, and I got a grip on myself.

The bailiff impression was intensified when he brought a wadge of official-looking documents out of his brief-case, and announced defiantly: 'You will see from these that I am acting within my rights in requesting you to hand over a certain article, which I have reason to believe was delivered here, some days ago.'

'Oh, not that old book carrier again?' I said crossly.

His eyes narrowed, giving him a passing resemblance to his late son: 'The article I refer to, madam, was the property of the late Arthur Brown. My information is that a suitcase, belonging to him, is concealed on these premises.'

'Would you oblige me by identifying the source of your information?' I asked, hoping to rattle him with a matching flow of jargon, and stalling like a madwoman.

I had a moment's fear that he would tell me it had come on the hot line from Heaven, which would have flummoxed me a bit, but he shook his head and looked more absurdly pompous than ever: 'Regret I am not empowered to divulge ...'

'In that case,' I said haughtily, as my feet touched firmer ground, 'I cannot accede to your request.'

'I think you will find the requisite authority here, madam,' he said, thrusting the papers under my nose. 'If you would be so good as to peruse them.'

There were two documents, both on solicitor's writing paper, and signed by two of the partners. The top one purported to be a copy of a clause from Julian's will, appointing his father joint executor. The other contained a terse request To Whom it Might Concern, to hand the bearer any property of Arthur Edwin Brown, deceased, for purposes of probate.

I pretended to take my time over reading them, but my thoughts were scurrying around like a cageful of mice. Since the old boy's information, thus far, had been accurate, and, since a shrewd business brain no doubt ticked away behind the ridiculous exterior, it behoved me neither to show my hand too early, nor to try any bluff which he might have the power to call.

However, the paramount need was to convince him that I was not alone in the house and, seized by an inspiration, I went to the foot of the stairs and called:

'Toby! Is Miss Montagu Dashwood there, Toby?' then, much louder: 'Sandy! Sandeee!'

There was a brief silence before her answering boom, and I shouted back: 'Don't bother to come down, but please ring up Scotland Yard and say that Robin is needed here, right away?'

'What's up?' she asked, blundering into view at the top of the stairs, her face grey with apprehension.

'Everything's okay, so don't worry, but I'd like Robin to come as soon as he can.'

I turned back to Mr Brown, switching on some rueful charm: 'I've asked them to send for my husband because I'm not sure what I ought to do. You've put me in a quandary, actually.'

'My dear young lady, if you are not satisfied with my credentials perhaps you would care to put through a personal call to the solicitors?'

'I didn't mean to suggest that the papers were forged, or anything. It's more a question of moral ethics, if you follow me.'

'No, I don't,' he said, understandably enough. 'I don't see where they come into it.'

'I must explain that I was storing this suitcase as a personal favour to your son. He was afraid of its falling into the wrong hands, and I promised faithfully not to give it up to anyone. How can I be sure that in letting you have it, I should be carrying out his wishes?'

'Very laudable sentiments, madam, but any arrangement you may have entered into with my son is automatically terminated by his death. As co-executor, I have complete jurisdiction over his property, unless otherwise specified.'

Of course, I had known this perfectly well, but a little more time had been wasted, and I reckoned that only a dash more beating around the bush would be required, to stall him off until Robin arrived.

'Is that so?' I asked, affecting great astonishment.

'You have my word for it. So, now, if I might trouble you ... I have many pressing matters to attend to.'

'Yes, I'm sure, but, unfortunately, there's still rather a big snag.'

'Indeed?'

'I can show you which cupboard the suitcase is in, but it's locked, and I haven't got the key.'

'I do not think that need delay us, madam.'

I had been afraid it wouldn't, having now formed the conclusion that he, possibly in collusion with Mr and Mrs Ted, had killed Julian for the express purpose of procuring this very key. However, my brain had not been idle during all the hanky panky, and, when he produced it from his waistcoat pocket, saying: 'Would this be the one in question?' I shook my head firmly.

'Oh no, nothing like it; much too small.'

He may have believed me, too, but I did not care. What mattered was that I had him stumped. I had guessed from the start that his embarrassment and petty civil service jargon sprang from unfamiliarity with human beings, and lack of practice in communicating with them, but that, within himself, he was sure of his ground. Even my cunningly contrived reference to Scotland Yard had not shaken him; but now his sagging jaw and bulging eyes told me that I had only to persist in my denial to achieve a permanent stalemate. In fact, I did better than this, I said: 'May I know what made you think that was the key?'

'That is my business.'

'I should think it is mine, too. I am not accustomed to people barging in,' I said, stretching a point, 'and producing some old key, as though that gave them the right to help themselves to anything in the house.'

'I received it through the post,' he admitted sullenly.

'Who from?'

'That I cannot say, but the ... message, which accompanied it, left me in no doubt that it was genuine. It confirmed certain facts which were already known to members of my family.'

'Nevertheless, you were misinformed. It is true that your son left a suitcase here, but the key to that cupboard is nothing like the one you have shown me. That's all I have to say.'

I can be very convincing, when I'm telling the direct lie, and I could see that I had him by the short hairs. Glaring at me venomously, his hand went once more to the brief-case:

'Very well. Here is the message I received. Read it for yourself.'

It was short and to the point, consisting of two sentences:

THE DIARIES ARE IN THE ALCOVE CUPBOARD AT TWELVE BEACON SQUARE. KEY ENCLOSED.

There was no signature and the message was printed, in capital letters, on a plain, buff, post office card.

(ii)

It goes without saying that Robin subsequently told me that I had been irresponsible, unethical and downright idiotic, but, to this day, I feel proud to remember how I won the game, with a card which I did not even know was a trump.

What happened was that, as I stood there, staring at the post-card, my mind shooting back to an evening when Robin had first described the complicated bus rides of Messrs X, B and A, a key turned in the front door, and Robin, himself, came bursting into the hall. I cannot imagine what pretext Sandy had used, but it must have been something fairly imaginative, for he had not even stopped to play the loudspeaker game. From the wild look in his eye, I concluded that he had been prepared to find me lying in a pool of blood.

'You all right?' he asked, the fever subsiding, as he took in the orderly scene.

'Fine, thanks. This is Mr Brown, Julian's father.'

'How do you do, sir? What can we do for you?'

'There's been a bit of a mix up,' I said, eager to get my version in first. 'Mr. Brown has come to collect the suitcase Julian left here. He tells me he's perfectly entitled to take it, but the trouble is, I haven't got a key to the cupboard, and the one he's brought wouldn't fit.'

I was winking laboriously, and striving to catch his eye, as I spoke, but it was lost to him, because he had snatched the postcard out of my hand, and his whole attention was fixed on that.

'When did you receive this?' he asked, turning to Mr Brown.

'By this morning's post, if you must know.'

'I must. What about the envelope?'

'Envelope?'

'I presume that the key was not attached to this card by a piece of string?'

'Oh no, quite so; it had slipped my mind. I destroyed it, I'm afraid.'

'Sure of that?' Robin snapped.

'What? Oh yes, positive.'

'Why?'

'If you doubt my word sir...'

'Why did you destroy it?'

'That's my business.'

'Is it? You mean, you had a reason?'

'No, no, not that; of course not. The fact is, it didn't occur to me. I just took the thing out of its envelope, along with my other letters, and I suppose it went into the waste-paper basket.'

'You suppose?'

'Well, that's the most likely thing.'

'Where was this? At your home, or your office?'

'At my home. My secretary deals with all the office mail.'

'You say it arrived this morning. What has happened to the waste-paper basket, in the meantime? Will it have been emptied?'

'I couldn't say. My daughter-in-law is in charge of all our domestic arrangements. I fail to see what purpose ...'

He tailed off uncertainly, for Robin had ceased to listen. He had lapsed into a dreamy silence, a wondering, faintly amused expression on his face. This gambit often proved effective. Having rattled the customer with an opening burst of machine-gun questions, he would wait for the first signs of grogginess, then retire into happy contemplation, as though all had been revealed to him, and he was free, once more, to get on with his stamp collection. Only witnesses with nerves of steel could survive the slackening of tension, or resist filling in the pregnant silence with an attempt at self-justification, and Mr Brown was not one of them.

'If you would just explain the purpose of all these questions, I am sure I should have no objection ...' he began, on a more cringing note, but Robin was not ready for him.

'Excuse me a moment,' he said absently, and walked away from us, into the dining-room. Leaving the door wide open, he crossed to the sideboard and picked up the telephone. He stood facing us as he dialled a number, cupping the mouthpiece with his hand so that his words did not reach us. During this interlude he did not once take his eyes off Mr Brown, and, when he replaced the receiver and returned to us, his manner was as placid as ever.

'Now, what about this key, sir? Had you seen it before?'

'No, never. Never until today.'

'I shall need to keep it, I'm afraid.'

'But, since you've admitted it's not your property. At least, your good lady here ...'

'What she said was, I believe, that it did not fit the lock in question, which is perfectly true.'

I had been desperately fighting for his attention, with another round of winks and nudges, all of which he blandly ignored; but, now, hearing my involuntary squeak of astonishment, turned to me at last, saying:

'As you've noticed, the lock has been changed. However, I have the new key with me, so we need not delay any longer.'

He had, too; a brand-new, brass key, about twice the length of the original.

'Shall we go and inspect this famous suitcase?' he asked in a chatty voice, heading for the drawing-room.

Mr Brown and I galloped along behind, and stood mesmerised, as he unlocked the alcove door. The suitcase was still inside.

'Look out!' I warned Robin, as he knelt down and grasped the handle. 'It weighs a ton!'

'Another of your famous exaggerations, I think,' he answered, lifting the case on to the carpet. 'Eight pounds would be nearer the mark. Would you care to open it, sir?'

'There's no call for that, as I can see,' Mr Brown said, fighting back. 'The contents are the private and personal property of my son.'

'Were.'

'Pardon?'

'I am afraid the joker who posted you that key was having you on. This has been a disappointing visit for you, and the worst of it is, I shall have to insist on the suitcase remaining here, for the time being, as well as the key and the postcard. Just hang on a minute, and I'll write you out a receipt for all three.'

Even I had now solved the enigma, but Mr Brown still lagged some way behind. He continued to protest that the case was his property and he was entitled to do as he pleased with it. Robin paid no attention. When he had finished writing he held out the sheet of paper, saying: 'I regret having to remind you of these distressing facts, but your son was murdered, and the police have still to find the criminal and bring him to trial. These articles may provide valuable evidence. They will be returned to you in due course, but I confess I am puzzled by your eagerness to possess yourself of one anonymous card, a key which fits nothing, and an empty suitcase of quite ordinary variety.'

'Empty? What do you mean? What about the diaries?'

'Gone, if they were ever there. See for yourself, if you wish,' Robin said, clicking open the case and dramatically throwing back the lid as he spoke.

Mr Brown stared incredulously, his eyes bulging and the beetroot flush slowly rising.

'They've been stolen! It's a trick! I've been tricked!'

'Too true,' Robin agreed cheerfully. 'It's a lesson to us all, isn't it?'

'What's that? What is?'

'Not to believe everything we read on anonymous postcards.'

(iii)

'You played it very cool,' I said later. 'Or did you know, all along, that the suitcase was empty?'

'Well, of course.'

'Since when?'

'Yesterday evening. After you and Toby left, I forced the lock. Well, look, darling, it was your idea that Julian was killed by someone who wanted to get his hands on the diary. We know that attempt failed, so what more logical than to assume Sebastian was murdered for the same reason? The first step was to find out if the diaries were still in the cupboard. They weren't, of course, but the case was there, and I had a hunch that we hadn't heard the last of it. That's why I got someone round to fix a new lock while you were upstairs with your little head buried in a script this morning.' He laughed, and added: 'It must have been quite a turn up for the book, when your romance about the key turned out to be the strict truth?'

'I acted for the best. Something had to be done to stall him until you arrived, and my intentions were honourable. That is very often the difference between my sort of falsehood and other people's.'

'It is a difference which is sometimes invisible to the naked eye.'

'This time, we have the postcard to vindicate me. We should never have winkled that out of him by straightforward methods. Do you suppose he sent it to himself, to account for having the key, but meaning only to fall back on it as a last resort?'

'If so, he's in big trouble. Murder suspect, and blackmailer, too.'

'Was it the same card as Betty got?'

'Ninety-nine per cent certain.'

'And Peter Hitchens, too, I suppose?'

'Yes. We found one among his papers.'

'I wonder if poor Peter can possibly have been the blackmailer, and then committed suicide in a fit of remorse? It doesn't seem in character, somehow, but they say that blackmailers often do send threatening letters to themselves. Some kind of schizophrenia, I suppose.'

'More often a purely practical attempt to divert suspicion.'

'Well, that doesn't apply, because there was no reason on earth why you should ever have suspected Peter. And, somehow, I can't see Mr Brown playing such a complicated game, either. He hasn't got the imagination for it. I did once toy with the idea that he'd knocked Julian off in order to provide himself with another contact in the spiritual world. But it was a bit far-fetched, and he can hardly have wanted Sebastian for that purpose.'

'And, if one of our theories is right, he must be innocent. He would not have murdered Sebastian just to get possession of the diaries, only to return the following day, with some cock and bull yarn about probate and anonymous postcards. On the other hand, we may be on the wrong track altogether. Perhaps we're over-estimating the importance of the diaries?'

It is always disagreeable to hear that any track one is on is a false one, and I said: 'No, I'm positive they're at the root of it, but, if you ask me, it was Lavender who sent the postcard.'

'Oh? Why her?'

'Well, assuming for the moment that she was the blackmailer, and, therefore, the murderer, she may have thought things were warming up, and, knowing what a goofy old party her father-in-law was, she deliberately set him up as the fall guy.'

'What expressions you pick up in movieland! Anyway, I suspect the only evidence you have against Lavender is that you and she had a slight misunderstanding over a book carrier.'

'Not at all. Her behaviour has been consistently odd, and lots of things point to her being your Mrs B. She was a great chum of Jasmine's, before and after the father's suicide, and she probably knew a hell of a lot more than most people what led up to it. Come to think of it, that vast sum she coughed up for Jasmine's hotel could have been conscience money. Yes, I think you could do worse than put Lavender under your lens.'

'And what about Sebastian? What was her motive there?'

'I'll need a few extra facts, before I can give you the complete reconstruction. For example, we don't know exactly when the diaries were removed. If it was before I went to Warwickshire, up crops Lavender again, with her book carrier. But yes, of course, Robin! I have it all now. She arrives here, with a book carrier in a suitcase, which is identical to the one she's seen Julian carrying out of the shop. She invents some tale to get Sebastian out of the house, unloads the parcel, switches suitcases and there you are! What could be simpler?'

'Lots of things. How did she get the key to our cupboard?'

'Oh, pinched it, while Julian was in the bath. I bet she could get into his flat any time she liked.'

'Still, she'd need to be quite a hefty girl. You warned me that the diaries weighed a ton. On the other hand, did you actually handle the case, when Julian brought it?'

'Not on your life. He wouldn't let anyone near it. He was like a tigress with her first-born.'

'So it could have been empty, even then? He was making heavy weather of it, just to fool you?'

'What would be the point? He was the one who was so crazy keen to hide the diaries here. If he'd told me he'd changed his mind, and brought along an empty case, I'd have been overjoyed.'

'But, having started the charade, to dupe his family, maybe, he might have felt it safer to keep it up with you?'

'Oh, that's much too complicated. Besides, he wasn't capable of putting on an act like that. I should have seen through it in a twink. No, I much prefer my Lavender theory; and, as for the case being too heavy for her, I'm not a bit bothered by that. She's a real, bony, peasant type.'

'With such a real, bony, peasant brain that she has to return, three days later, and murder Sebastian, just for the hell of it?'

'No; for the most cogent of reasons. Probably he came back, while she was in the throes of her suitcase switching, and guessed what she was up to. Or she thought he had. He may even have caught her in the act. How about that? Then she'd not only have to silence him, but actually finish the job. So she seized the chance of my being away to make a return visit.'

'She was taking her time, wasn't she? She can hardly have relied on Sebastian's being so co-operative as to keep his mouth shut until the time was propitious for killing him. He never mentioned anything about it to you, did he?'

'No,' I said sadly. 'But there are indications that

Sebastian was playing a little game of his own, which might have induced him to keep quiet.'

I described the disturbing revelations of the passport photograph, and how it followed that, in going to the drawer to collect my brooch, Sebastian must have seen the diary. Robin agreed that it was unlikely that he would have resisted taking a peep.

'That could be the reason his room was ransacked,' I went on. 'Lavender had first to kill him, and then to search his room for any bits of the diary which he might have extracted for his own use.'

Robin cautioned me about getting a closed mind where Lavender was concerned. He added that a nice, innocuous little job, which I could more profitably engage in, was writing out a detailed description of the brooch, for circulation both here and in Holland, although I warned him that it would be a waste of time, since I could never bear to look at the thing again.

The argument was brought to a close by Sandy, who had finished loading up the camping gear, and had popped in to wish us Nighty-bye, chaps, and to be of Good cheer.

'Like me to give you Friday of this week, as well?' she asked. 'Many hands, and all that?'

'Oh, Sandy, I'd love it, but what about your real Friday job?'

'Not to worry. She can go to Hades, if you'll pardon my French.'

'You see what I mean about Sandy?' I asked Robin, when we were alone again. 'She not only copes with every boring job under the sun, but she throws in half a dozen gems from her repertoire, every time she comes here. It's what I call the rich, full life, or two for the price of one.'

Nineteen

Without any doubt, it was my close and intimate relationship with the telephone which provided the key to every puzzle. A small anomaly connected with Robin's front-door gadget, plus a psychological slip of the tongue on Toby's part added their contribution, but it was my long experience of the telephone, in all its moods, which clinched matters.

Not that I was able to act upon my knowledge as rapidly as the situation demanded. By the time we went to bed that Wednesday night, all the separate strands were in my hands. I need only have devoted myself, for a few hours, to the job of weaving them into the right pattern for the solution to be spread out before us; but two factors caused a postponement. One was outside my control, the other concerned a supposition I had formed, for which confirmation was needed from another source.

Unfortunately, the first got in the way of the second, for, early on Thursday morning my agent telephoned to ask if I had read the script, and if it had found favour. It was typical of her that she did not refer to the trifling matter of a bloody murder, which had just occurred in the client's kitchen; but the fact was that, until she knew for certain whether this event was the portender of good or adverse publicity, her interest in it remained, to put it mildly, in abeyance.

I responded to her inquiries in ringing tones, and she told me that a high-powered conference had been convened, in a suite at the Dorchester at eleven o'clock, at which my presence was required.

I suggested a rendezvous at her office, so that we could make our entrance together, but she was in no mood to risk my breaking my neck on the journey between Beacon Square and Park Lane, and informed me that she had already hired a car for me from our local garage.

Naturally this development took precedence over all other considerations, and I should barely have noticed if the new cook-housekeeper had served up prussic acid, instead of coffee, on my breakfast tray. In justice, I might add that she did nothing of the sort, but as she also proved to be far less accomplished than Sebastian in helping me choose what to wear, even hinting that she did not consider it to be a matter of overwhelming importance, it would have taken more than this purely negative virtue to endear her to me.

I was not over sanguine about the forthcoming meeting, because, as we all know, only the big stars can set up their own productions. The rest of us have to rub along with what we're given, and be thankful it's no worse. Inevitably, there were certain aspects of this one which I could have done without, but I kept quiet about them, and worked away like a beaver at being keen and co-operative, and everybody's darling. Unlike Wordsworth, I take the view that the good, sweet maid is also the clever one.

The real trouble was that the argy bargy went on until after one o'clock, and I was flattened with exhaustion by the end of it. Neither the time nor the mood was suitable for a spurious shopping expedition, which was the next item of my schedule.

My agent advised me to go home and sleep it off, and, to save argument, I pretended to fall in with the idea.

However, as we circled Trafalgar Square, I asked the driver to change direction and drop me off in the Haymarket. The closer we got to Beacon Square, the stronger grew my aversion to spending an afternoon there. It was not simply the prospect of the sour-faced house-keeper, so different from silly, prattling Sebastian, which daunted me; there was an actual physical queasiness to be reckoned with, as well. Allowing it to rule me, I alighted from the car, walked into the nearest cinema, and bought a seat in the lower depths of the dim and cavernous auditorium, which is probably the nearest modern equivalent to a good curl up in the womb.

(ii)

I was reborn, blinking into the sunlight, at about five o'clock, and took a taxi to Thurgoods. Business appeared to be normal on the ground floor, with sales of biscuit tins and rocking chairs as brisk as ever, but it was a different story in the antiques department.

'Most of my customers are regulars,' Betty explained. 'I suppose they feel it would be indelicate to intrude on our grief. Silly fools! A bit of turnover would do my grief all the good in the world. Have you come to buy something?'

'In a way, yes.'

'Splendid! What, in particular?'

'Oh, any old thing. Just so long as it costs the regulation twenty-five smackers.'

She eyed me morosely: 'Now, what are you up to?'

'Nothing special. I've had a gruelling session with the tycoonery, and you know how thirsty one begins to feel by about five-thirty?'

'Thirsty for what?'

'Okay, if you must know, there are a couple of points I want to clear up with Barnes. What are you beefing about? I thought you were burning to make a sale?'

She sat down at her desk and fitted some carbons into the sales pad: 'Not that kind.'

'What are you doing?'

'Making out a bogus receipt for one Staffordshire dog, price twenty-seven pounds. There'll be hell to pay with the auditors, when the day of reckoning comes, but who cares? God knows what mischief you're brewing, but I don't intend to stand by and watch you throw your money away, as well. Here's your copy.'

'The bar continues to function?' I asked, as we travelled up in the lift.

'So far, though not many takers nowadays.'

Her words were borne out by the desolate scene which greeted us on the second floor. Barnes was alone in his corner of the room, but without the usual evening paper in evidence. He was huddled over a radio, which whispered the racing results in his ear. He was fortunate to have such an engrossing hobby, and he did not look particularly pleased to be interrupted in it, evidently holding different views from Betty on the usefulness of intruders into grief.

'Your usual, madam?' he inquired, in a pained voice, when the ritual with my bill had been concluded.

'No, don't bother with that,' I told him. 'Just a tomato juice. I really came to thank you for your tip for the Oaks. I trust you backed it yourself?'

He had turned, to reach for a glass on the shelf behind him, and I saw his back stiffen.

'I am afraid I do not recall, madam.'

'Oh, really? I know a lot has happened, to put it out of your mind, but you'd watched the race on television, by that time, hadn't you? Still, no matter. There was another thing I wanted to ask you about that day.'

'Indeed, madam?' he asked, in a frozen voice, 'I am sure I cannot think what else there'd be as you'd want to know.'

'I am sure you couldn't,' I agreed, 'until I've asked you,' and I did so.

He gave a flat negative, so I put the question in a different form, and, this time, a shadow of hesitation prefaced his denial. I rephrased it once more, and reluctantly he admitted that it might be so.

'Thanks very much,' I said, downing the tomato juice. 'That's all I wanted to know.'

'Just as well I stayed glued,' Betty remarked, as we descended. 'I think he'd have gone for you with the ice pick, if I hadn't been a witness. What were you driving at, anyway, with all that taradiddle about race meetings and people getting into lifts?'

'Just a little theory of mine,' I answered nonchalantly. 'A correct one, too, to judge by the way things are falling into place.'

'You ought to watch it,' she said, alighting at the first floor. 'You're on dangerous ground, you know, and you might not have me around to protect you, next time. If you ask me, the best thing those tycoons of yours could do is set you to work, in the profession in which it has pleased God to call you.'

'You sound just like Robin,' I said.

'Do I now? Well, there are worse ways of sounding, I daresay. Still, I suppose there isn't the faintest hope of your listening to either of us.'

'Cheer up!' I said. 'We're nearly at the end of the line now. All our troubles will soon be over,' and, pushing the button, swooped out of sight.

The assurance had been the slightest bit premature,

for there were still one or two unpleasant developments in store, but, unfortunately, I can never resist an exit line.

Twenty

Sandy arrived late on Friday morning, for the first and only time in our acquaintance, and I began to wonder if she had thought better of her offer, or if Bobs had applied the veto. I was watching for the red Mini, from the upstairs sitting-room, when I saw, or thought I saw, Toby's car in the street below. However, it drove slowly by and turned out of the Square, and I reminded myself that there must be dozens of ancient green Mercedes floating around London.

A few minutes later, Sandy arrived on foot, with a tale of woe to account for her unpunctuality, and many a hearty oath.

'Blast and Botheration take it!' she grumbled, trundling her great weight upstairs. 'Grovelling apologies and all that, old Scout, but some yob had to drive straight into my rear, at the traffic lights. Going much too fast, as I told him, in no uncertain terms.'

'Hard cheese!' I said. 'Much damage?'

'Might have been worse, but there's a flipping great dent, and one of the lights was smashed. I dropped it off at the garage round the corner, and finished the journey on Shanks's P.'

'Can they fix it?'

'Hope so. Bobs will be sick as mud, otherwise. We'd promised ourselves an outing to Burnham Beeches tomorrow, if the weather holds, and public transport is just not on these days.'

'Well, don't despair,' I told her. 'We use that garage

a lot, as you know, and I might be able to pull a string or two.'

'Thanks muchly. Knew I could count on you to come to the aid of the party, as per. Well, now, mustn't stand here gassing. What's on the agenda for this morning?'

'Plenty,' I assured her. 'First, something has to be done about Sebastian's insurance cards, etcetera. I've no idea what, but doubtless you have. There are about a thousand letters, too, and do you think you could wheedle that dragon in the kitchen into giving us an early lunch? I have to be at the Studios by two, and that means leaving here at one sharp.'

I gave her a report on the Dorchester conference, and said that I had an appointment with the Wardrobe Department at two o'clock.

Sandy undertook to cope with it all, but asked if she might first telephone Bobs, to put her in the picture about the Mini situation. I told her that permission was granted as soon as asked.

I did not remain in the room while she made the call, for I had a fancy to test a theory, which Sebastian had once propounded, concerning eavesdropping on telephone conversations. His notion had been that the safest method was to pick up the extension while the other person was still dialling, as, at this stage, the extra click was unnoticeable. Having embarked on the experiment, I was obliged to listen to the entire conversation, lest the second click should give the game away. It was rather fascinating.

Later on, I walked round to the delicatessen, and stocked up with pate and cheese and so forth, with which I hoped to soften the dragon's wrath when she was asked to serve lunch an hour before schedule.

My next call was at the garage, to order a car for the

afternoon, and inspect the damaged Mini. I engaged in a friendly chat with the foreman, whose name was Charlie and was every inch my darling, and, just as I was leaving, I caught another glimpse of the Mercedes, parked in an alley beside the garage. I turned back, meaning to ask Charlie if it really was Toby's, but he had his head and shoulders inside an engine by then, and it was not worth the trouble of extricating him.

I warned Sandy that the outlook was not bright: 'I did my best,' I assured her. 'But there seems to be some internal damage, as well. They have to get a new part, and it may not be in until late this afternoon. Don't faint, though, Sandy, because I've told you the worst bit first. The good news is that they've promised to have it ready some time this evening, and Charlie will deliver it to you, in person, all furbished up for Burnham Beeches.'

'Oh, blessings on you! What a trump you are!'

'And that's not all, because I can easily drop you off at your flat, on my way to the Studios. Ealing is practically next door.'

Sandy was loud in her rejoicing, and I was not dissatisfied, either. Altogether a creditable performance, I considered, for one who was necessarily out of practice. I put the final artistic touch to it, by attiring myself in the sort of outfit I would actually have worn, had I been contemplating a visit to the Wardrobe Department.

Emerging from the house at ten minutes to one, I spoke a few words to the constable on duty outside our house, and then took my place beside Sandy in the hired car.

The traffic thinned out as we came up from the Hyde Park Corner tunnel, and a clock on the corner of Sloane Street gave the time as twelve minutes past.

'Loads of time,' I said, but Sandy had turned her head to look at Harrods' window. So far I had made all the running, and I was curious to know at which point she would take over. It had not happened by the time we halted at some traffic lights at Hammersmith, and, as we shot forward again, I said: 'Perhaps you should give the driver some directions? I only told him that we wanted an address in Ealing.'

She leant forward, wound down the glass panel, and gabbled some instructions in the driver's ear. He nodded, without taking his eyes off the road, or slackening speed. The slight exertion took its toll of Sandy, who lurched back into her seat, her face scarlet and her eyes watering. It took her five or six minutes to regulate her breathing, in which we covered almost as many miles. Then the driver slowed down and turned into a cul-de-sac, not much bigger than a yard, and she cleared her throat noisily.

'Is this where you live?' I asked. 'How very nice and secluded!'

'Since you're here, at last,' she croaked, after another deafening round with the vocal chords, 'how about coming in for a sec, to say Hallo to Bobs? She'd be thrilled to the marrow.'

The phrasing was in her usual style, but all the heartiness had oozed away, and the words came out in a jerky splutter. I knew that she had been turning over these, and other simple sentences, ever since we left Beacon Square.

'Perhaps that would be best,' I said. 'Since I understand I am expected.'

My reply had also received its measure of silent rehearsal, but training counts, and tone and delivery were gratifyingly controlled.

Taking an envelope from my bag, I said to the

driver: 'I shall only be ten minutes; please read this, while you're waiting.'

In a desperate hurry all of a sudden, Sandy had lumbered across the pavement, and was inside the building before I caught up with her. She made for the staircase and started up it, without turning to see whether I followed or not. It cost me an effort to do so, for part of me longed to bolt for the safety of the car; but pride, as much as curiosity, kept me going Despite all her practice, she was more out of breath than I was when I came alongside her on the third floor, and I had enough of mine left to observe pleasantly: 'Must be quite a job, getting the wheel chair up all these stairs?'

Without answering, or meeting my look, she unlocked the door and walked inside. I followed her into a box-like hall, where a number of suitcases were stacked against a wall, and, from there, into a room beyond it.

'We're here,' she called out, in a flat, dead voice. Then, wheeling round to face me at last, her chest heaving and her face ashen, she added: 'Let me introduce you to Bobs.'

A small, hunched figure occupied a chair facing the door. One bony little hand fondled the ears of a snapping terrier, curled on his lap, and his hooded, amber eyes blinked malevolently up at me: 'Come into my parlour,' he said softly.

It was not a bad line, in the circumstances; but he could equally well have said: 'Welcome to Toad Hall.'

(ii)

'I should warn you,' I said, 'that dozens of people know I am here, and the driver has instructions to come and break down your door, if I'm not out in ten minutes.'

'Sit down, please. I don't like looking up at people.'

I daresay he had had a surfeit of it. Sandy, being more conversant with the rules, was already slumped in a chair between me and the door.

'Is this true?' he asked her, and she answered heavily: 'I don't know. Everything got out of hand. Not my fault.'

At least one impression I had gathered over the months had not been false. Whatever their relationship might really be, Sandy was totally dominated by Bobs, and her manner now, in the face of his displeasure, was abject.

'What a clumsy fool you are!' he told her contemptuously. 'I guessed you'd bungled it, when I heard she was bringing you here, of her own accord. Why the hell couldn't you see it?'

'Don't blame her,' I said. 'I am sure your instructions were carried out to the letter, as usual. Only this time, I took a leaf from your book and overheard them. After that, I preferred to play it my way.'

'You mean, you listened in?' Sandy asked, flushing with anger, or mortification. I daresay criminals are invariably shocked by dishonourable practices on the part of law-abiding citizens. It must make them feel so insecure.

'To every word; starting with the report that the Mini had been duly bashed up, as the prelude to getting me to drive you out here. That's why I thought it would be nicer to lay it on, myself, with a driver who knows me. Don't look so shocked. Eavesdropping must seem quite natural to you; not to mention Sebastian. Did he try a little counter-blackmail, or did he just threaten to expose you? Poor Sebastian, I should like to think it was that. Anyway, when I heard you both cooking up ways to trick me into coming here, I decided to be one jump ahead, and I am; several, in fact.'

I tried to sound confident, but I was not happy to see that Bobs's burst of temper had passed, and there was even a gleam of amusement in his cold, unwavering stare.

'You could have saved yourself the trouble, girlie. In fact, the present arrangement suits me very well. Evidently, you consider yourself to be quite clever, but I must disillusion you. You say that dozens of people know you are here. Who, for instance?'

'Actually, I only told one, but that's a technicality, because he was the policeman outside our house. He'll have passed on my message by now, though; so dozens of people do know.'

'Very prudent of you. What address did you give him?'

'Why, this one, naturally.'

His amusement increased: 'I think not. Perhaps you are not so many jumps ahead as you thought. We moved out of the old flat two days ago.'

'I don't believe you,' I said, meaning the reverse.

'It is immaterial. Time will show which of us is right. And we're still in Ealing, let me add. Such a clever girlie as you might have been able to tell the difference between that, and, let us say, Balham. But Ealing covers a large area, and the old flat is several miles away. I am afraid that when your friends arrive at the address you gave them, they will find no one there. They will learn that the arthritic old lady, who used to live there has moved to a nursing home, and the cheerful, devoted daughter has not been back either. Our neighbour, Mrs Goldsmith, is a great chatterbox, and they are sure to get the full story from her. It will be several hours, I daresay, before they pick up the trail again; more than enough for my purpose, I assure you.'

'There is still the driver,' I reminded him.

'Ah! So there is! Lucky you mentioned it. Ten minutes, I think you said? So he may come at any moment. But then, how is the poor fellow to find the right door?'

'He'll find it,' I said, trying to sound convincing. 'At least, he won't give up until he does.'

'But that might take half an hour, and I can't spare the time. No, I have a better idea.' His pebbly eyes shifted for a moment: 'Why not go down, yourself, Monica, and bring him up? Say that Mrs Price is asking for him. I expect he knows you quite well, and will not take it amiss. You could get out some beer first; he may be thirsty, poor lad.'

Sandy obediently lumbered to her feet, her face set and expressionless. I had tried, once or twice, to catch her eye, while the Toad was holding forth, but she had refused to meet mine. All the old ebullience had vanished, and she had become a lifeless puppet, slack and crumpled, until Master twitched the strings.

Although any faint hopes of her affection for myself being genuine had long been dissipated, none the less her departure added painfully to my growing uneasiness. There was a wickedness about the Toad, so blatant as to be almost tangible. The atmosphere of the ugly little room was loaded with it, and this, combined with his repellent looks and sneering manner, was oppressing me almost beyond bearing.

'What are you going to do?' I forced myself to ask.

He blinked at me, affecting surprise: 'Why, nothing, girlie, I sincerely hope. It is what you are going to do that is important.'

'I should have thought that was obvious. As soon as the driver comes, I shall say that I wish him to take me home, at once. I shall also warn him not to drink the beer, or anything else that is offered him, since it probably contains a Micky Finn, if not worse.'

He shook his head wearily: 'You still think this is a game, don't you? But I expect you'll learn. Begin with this lesson: when the chauffeur comes, you will tell him that you have altered your plans. Your friends will be driving you home, later. He is to take the car back to the garage. Got that?'

'Why should I?' I asked, with a sinking heart, knowing that he would tell me.

'Because if you utter one word outside those instructions, the driver will not be taking the car anywhere at all. He will not get up off this floor until his body is found some time tomorrow, or the day after, maybe, and is carried out to the mortuary. Poor fellow, he won't even know what struck him. Wife and little ones waiting at home, too, I daresay.'

This last contemptible reflection so inflamed me that it restored a flicker of life to my failing spirits.

'You've left out the widowed mother,' I said. 'And, if you think you can get away with it, you must be raving mad.'

'I shall get away with it; have no fears on that score. I am not an idiot, like yourself. But you were quite right to refuse my bait; I'll grant you that much. Saving the chauffeur's life would not really have prolonged your own. You're too much of a risk. It might have been more convenient to take you out of here alive, but one can't always have everything just the way one wants it, can one?'

'What does all that mean? Where are you taking me?'

'Naturally, you are curious. Well, it's not very far; I can tell you that much. We are leaving, ourselves, quite soon, you know. The plane goes at four. But, luckily, there is quite a convenient stretch of water between here and Heathrow. As soon as I have dealt with, ah ... immediate business, we shall load up the luggage, and any other encumbrances, and be on our way. The car is parked outside, incidentally; a Bentley, with quite a capacious boot. One of the compensations for what, in some respects, can be a tedious profession. Ealing is handy for the airport, admittedly, but it has its dull side. But you'll be pleased to hear, girlie, that your little treats gladdened our lives no end. Many's the good laugh we've had over them. It was so comically naive of you to imagine you could bribe my wife with little titbits from your larder. It's true that you saved us a journey or two to Harrods; but, you see, my dear, she had no intention of leaving your delightful household, so long as it provided us with something useful. In the way of business, I mean.'

I gazed at him with stunned loathing, the full realisation of my stupid complacency dawning on me, at last, and, paradoxically, stirred, as I had not been before, by a passionate wish to outwit this repulsive creature. Threatening to kill me was one thing; making a fool of me, quite another.

Misinterpreting my look, he said: 'You are still not sure whether to believe me? Understandable, perhaps. To allay any foolish doubts that I do mean business, I suggest you take a look out of the window. You will see the Bentley parked just down on the left.'

I walked, a little dizzily, over to the window. Strictly speaking, I was in no mood to appreciate Bentleys, with or without capacious boots, but any activity was preferable to crouching like a rabbit, while the snake went ranting on.

It was a sash window, and, to steady myself, I slung

the strap of my bag over my wrist, gripped the brass catches and pressed my forehead against the cool of the pane. From that vantage point, the whole of the little street was visible, and I could just see Sandy's back, as she leant inside the car, talking to the driver. I turned my head to the left, and, sure enough, a few yards away, there was a large, new-looking black Bentley.

I changed direction and stared across at the warehouse opposite, picturing all the normal, unsuspecting and indifferent people inside it, but not one of them answered my silent prayer to show himself. My gaze shifted to the street again, searching desperately for a stray pedestrian, or even a child playing; but, instead, from the corner of my eye, I perceived something else, which made my heart leap up much higher than if I had seen a rainbow in the sky. On the far side of the cul-de-sac, at the corner of the main road, was an old green Mercedes.

It was a moment for quick thinking and even quicker action, and I had no time for carefully constructed plans. Moving only my head, I took a slow look round. The Toad had not taken his eyes off me; I had felt them boring into me, as I stood there. They met mine, in a cruel, triumphant stare, and I knew that I would have only a few seconds to work in.

Nevertheless, his chair was a yard or two from the window, and the snarling little dog was still curled on his lap. Praying with all my soul that the sash would not stick, I tightened my hold on the two brass levers. Then I filled my lungs with air, flung up the window, and, with all the power I could command, let out a wild and piercing scream. With such force as still remained to me, I hurled my bag as hard and far as I could.

I did not even see where it landed, for it was still in flight when a hand covered my mouth, something struck my head with the force of a cannon-ball, and I pitched down into chasms of darkness.

Twenty-one

'It still leaves a lot to be explained,' Robin said, closing the wine list.

'I am so glad it was you who said that, and not I,' Toby replied. 'Now I can stop pretending that I understand anything at all.'

Ostensibly, the occasion was a celebration dinner, to mark my return to the sequestered life of the film studios; and there could be no doubt that their congratulations were sincere. But it was also the first time the three of us had been together, since the arrest of Mr and Mrs Phelps Sanderson, and the events which had led up to it still absorbed us all.

'Me, too,' I agreed, 'and I have to tell you that the biggest puzzle of all is the inexplicable behaviour of Toby.'

'Inexplicable nothing. If it weren't for Toby, you wouldn't be going back to work tomorrow. Personally, I can never be grateful enough for that small fact alone.'

'Oh, I've no wish to be churlish, but, having trailed me to that ghastly flat, why the cliff-hanging? Why didn't you come up and rescue me?'

'Because I am a dreadful coward,' he answered sadly.

'Rubbish! Can't you understand, Tessa, that, the minute he set foot in the flat, he'd not only have been in the same pickle as you, but useless to us, as well?'

'You can't expect me to see it in the same light,' I complained. 'All I know is that, while I was up there, fighting for my life, and damn near losing, old Toby was lolling back in the Mercedes.'

'Oh no, he wasn't. He's being too modest, altogether. The fact is that, having managed to keep on your tail all the way from Beacon Square, he then did the intelligent thing of knocking up some people in the corner house, and using their telephone to let me know where you were. As it happened, our men were still on their way to the old address, so we were able to divert them, in time. Otherwise, you'd have been a goner. No, it's not Toby's conduct which I criticise, it's your own. What, in the name of God, induced you to walk into their trap? Not only walk into it, but actually set it up for them?'

'Well, I heard them planning everything on the telephone. It made me so mad to think of them preening themselves on their own cleverness, and my gullibility, that I decided to play it my way.'

'Rather an expensive form of revenge.'

'How was I to know? I'd have kept well clear of them, if I'd known that killing me was included in the deal. I thought they might be accessories to murder, but nothing worse. In fact, I knew that Sandy couldn't have killed Julian, because she was in the room with me, when it happened. When Barnes finally came clean, I saw just how the murder had been worked, but that only confirmed Sandy's innocence; and I hadn't an inkling that Bobs and the Toad were one and the same.'

'Barnes's story, and he was quite positive about it, was that, as soon as the three remaining people in the Boardroom had gone down, he shut up shop, set the locking catch on the lift, and went off duty. After that, and until he returned, no one could have gone up to that floor without the special key, all of which were accounted for.'

'Yes, and I daresay he didn't mean to deceive you, but you don't know Barnes as I do. I bet you that, the moment those three walked towards the lift, he was back with the horses again. With all the hurly burly which old Peregrine had created, Barnes had scarcely had a moment for his real business. My guess is that he was on the line to his bookie before the lift gates even closed. He'd certainly have been in no frame of mind to notice that only two people got in, while the third sidestepped into the Gents, next door. As for Peregrine and Joannie, Barnes admits that they were both so stoned by then that they were probably seeing six people where there was only one, anyway.'

'They both insisted that the third person, the anonymous, cash-paying customer, went down with them.'

'You may be sure they did; although not to provide him with an alibi, but themselves. I bet that neither of them had any clear recollection of events, when they woke up the next morning and learnt that Julian had been murdered, within minutes of their leaving. No doubt, they were thankful to grab at any old witness, to back up their story.'

'While, in fact, the dreaded Singleton Bates had darted into the Gentlemen's Powder Room?' Toby asked.

'Yes; it's just beside the lift, you see. And, once in there, he could take his time. You can get down from the second floor, just by lifting a catch. It's only for coming up that you need the special key. He only had to stay there until he heard Julian arrive, which he did by appointment, presumably, since he hadn't turned up to meet Jasmine.'

Robin nodded: 'They've admitted that he wangled an appointment, on the pretext of possessing information concerning a certain Mrs Phelps Sanderson, formerly governess to the family of the late General Hawkes.'

'Julian could never have resisted that bait. I guessed that Sandy must have been involved, in some way, but I never thought of Bobs being her husband. What was the point of that arthritic mother business, anyway?'

'Precisely the one you've mentioned. Who would associate murder and blackmail with a poor old invalid woman? He had other disguises, but that was the one they mainly used. Betty had never seen him in her life, incidentally, which made it quite safe for him to play the A for Accomplice role, in her case. However, even though you didn't suspect them of murder, you did realise that Sandy was up to no good, and why you didn't inform the police, like any sane person, absolutely beats me.'

'I had no evidence; only my sixth and seventh senses, which they wouldn't have listened to. I had to force her to commit herself. In other words, I laid a trap for them; and, by planting the driver outside their flat, and telling our constable at Beacon Square where I'd gone, I thought I'd covered all the risks. Rash of me, I admit, because I'd tuned into Sandy, by then, and I knew there was something fishy.'

'You really knew, or was it just a lucky guess?'

'No, I really did. It was the mighty telephone which gave the clue, and I ought to have picked it up much sooner.'

'I've lost the thread again,' Toby said, appealing to Robin. 'Have you any idea what this is all about?'

'Not a glimmer.'

'It's quite simple. What happened was that, after Julian had rung up and burbled on in that strange way, Sandy tried to call him back on his private line. She talked me into letting her do it and she kept the receiver jammed against her ear until right at the end, just before she hung up. What I heard, in those two seconds, was the engaged signal. I had a nagging feeling, even then, that something was terribly wrong, but I was worrying about Julian, and I couldn't pin it down.'

'Pin what down?'

'Well, don't you see? Sandy had told me there was no reply, so what I ought to have heard was the ringing tone. It's a completely different signal, and would have altered the whole situation. So what was her reason for lying about it? In fact, the line was engaged, in so far as it had fallen out of Julian's hand and was dangling loose; but Sandy's job was to convince me that he was not in his office at all. In that way, she was giving the Toad time to finish the job and covering his retreat.'

'Well, I suppose so,' Robin said. 'But it was rather a frail platform to base her guilt on. It could have been a genuine mistake.'

'Oh, not with Sandy. You know as well as I do how rarely she made mistakes of that kind. In fact, it was the inadvertent mistake she made later on being so out of character that gave me my third pointer. You remember, when we came back from the Pub, the day after Sebastian's murder, and she made such a hash of opening the door to us?'

'Yes, but even you can't call that particularly significant. It was the first time she'd used the thing.'

'I know it was, but it shouldn't have been; that's the point. A bit earlier, she'd told us that Toby had brought some tax papers round, and, after the way you'd dinned it into us, I knew jolly well that he'd have made a terrible commotion, if she hadn't gone through the proper ritual. So how could she have muffed it a second time? It was too uncharacteristic not to have some meaning; and I bet you didn't come to the house at all that morning, did you, Toby?'

He shook his head: 'I was expecting you at the hotel for lunch, but she rang up and told me that you were both going off somewhere, for the whole afternoon, and would ring me in the country. A broad hint that I'd outstayed my welcome and it was time to draw stumps. Though why I had to be bundled out of the way is just one more thing that escapes me.'

'Perhaps it was simply that she wanted to clear the decks for action; but she may have realised that you, as well as I, were catching up with her. She was certainly getting rattled. For one thing, she was beginning to ham up her jolly old scoutmistress act rather excessively. I can't stand over-acting; it always makes me jumpy. I daresay she'd pigeon-holed you as the vacillating old ostrich, and gambled on the fact that, once you were safely tucked away in the country, it would be ages before the head came out of the sand. Long enough, anyway, for them to get to Brazil, or wherever it was. A grave error of judgement, as it turned out.'

'Altogether, she seems to have been a lot less astute than we gave her credit for,' Robin remarked. 'I believe they both went a bit wild, towards the end. Planting the book carrier in Sebastian's room was an unnecessary touch, and sending the key and postcard to old Brown was an even sillier elaboration. Our chaps got their hands on the envelope, and we'd have traced them through that, eventually.'

'Eventually,' I repeated, in a meaning voice.

'I am afraid that Tessa and I are partly to blame for their getting above themselves,' Toby said. 'We encouraged her to treat us like half-wits. It's such an easy way to get someone else to do all the boring jobs, but she swallowed it whole. She honestly thought that she only had to fob me off with some fatuous message, and I'd go trotting back to the country and settle down with my jigsaw.'

'Whereas, you found a more amusing game of tag, in London?'

'Well, to be fair, she did fob me off with her fatuous message, but I found it difficult to concentrate on the jigsaw, and I became fobbed on again; so, on Friday, I drove back to London. I'm not quite sure why. I had no proof, you know, any more than Tessa, that she was up to no good; but I thought it would be rather dashing to lurk about for a bit, and keep an eye on things. The shaming thing is that, after all, she nearly fooled me. So long as her horrid little car was not outside your house, I imagined there was nothing to worry about. It was purely the fluke of running out of petrol that made me spot it at the garage, and which put fresh heart into me, if you care to put it that way.'

'I'm proud of you,' I said. 'I can't help it, I really am.'

'What was your second clue, Tessa, when you've dried your eyes? I noticed that, in your typically maddening way, you jumped from number one to number three.'

'The middle one was another of Toby's contributions. He used to refer to Sandy by any old name that came into his head, but, on one memorable occasion, he called her Montagu Dashwood, and that was so odd.'

'Any odder than all the rest?'

'Much, because, you see, it was practically her right name. It shot me back about twenty years, and I remembered that the Hawkes governess was called Monica Dashwood. You must have heard it in those days, too, Toby. Was it sheer coincidence, or had you already made the connection?'

'I doubt if we'll ever know,' he replied. 'The workings of my mind are sometimes a little too subtle even for me to follow. Perhaps I said it first, and thought of it afterwards.'

'It seems to be a family weakness,' Robin remarked.

'It is not my only one,' Toby said plaintively. 'I am a coward, too, and not altogether bright. I have still not grasped the nub.'

'Which nub?'

'I hope there is not more than one. That would make me feel more foolish than ever. Why did her husband find it necessary to kill Julian at all?'

'They must have been afraid he'd recognised her. She knew him the minute he came into our drawing-room, she being that same little governess he'd cultivated all those years ago when she started her nefarious career. She had the advantage of a second or two, because, at first, he was too busy fussing over his silly old suitcase to take in anything else. So she plastered a handkerchief over her face and bolted, pretending there was some crisis with Bobs. But, of course, she couldn't be certain that he hadn't recognised her, and I expect she and the Toad decided that it was better to be safe than sorry. Later on, she probably thought that he'd not only recognised her, but passed the knowledge on to me. She had every reason to think so, because, when old Mr Brown came to collect the suitcase, I tried an experiment. I stood in the hall, shouting out names at random, and one of them was Montagu Dashwood. It was near enough to the real thing to give her a heart attack, and, I promise you, it damn near did. I thought she was going to fall straight down the stairs. She was frightened sick. I expect it was then that she decided I knew, or suspected, too much for my own good.'

'You behaved very rashly all round, as far as I can see; but you go too fast for me. To get back to my lovely old nub for a moment, surely she must have known who Julian was? You'd told her all about the job; didn't you mention her prospective employer?'

'You bet I did, with bells on. And I've no doubt that my graphic description of the Thurgood Boardroom, with its many quaint features, was most helpful to them in plotting the murder. But, you see, I didn't once refer to him as Julian Brown, which is the only name she would have known. It wasn't altogether an accidental omission. I really didn't intend to give away the whole show about his double identity, before she'd agreed to take him on. All she got from me was that he was a rich businessman, a director of Thurgoods, in fact, and that he was writing his autobiography, in diary form. When she'd known him, in his gilded youth, he was just plain Julian Brown, London's most dedicated socialite. It wasn't until years later that even his closest friends knew about the business side. I knew him moderately well, at one point, and I promise you I never had an inkling.'

'Yes, I remember your telling me that,' Robin said thoughtfully. 'And, naturally, she wouldn't have questioned you about his private life. The mere mention of diaries was quite enough to whet her appetite.'

'First-rate, potential blackmail material,' I agreed. 'And that, of course, was the real reason for taking on so many different jobs. As soon as she found herself in one that was leading nowhere, she made Bobs the excuse to back out. I'm appalled to remember what a rich vein she struck with us, and how easy we made it for her. Poor Peter Hitchens, for example. He was always ringing up with some heart-rending tale about his private life, and I suppose Sandy was on the extension, taking it all down in shorthand, for purposes of extortion?'

'I'm afraid that's true,' Robin said. 'As you know, they found one of those postcards among his belongings. It had me worried for a bit, I can tell you, because the only common denominator I could find between him and Betty was yourself. However, he was a real neurotic, you know, Tessa, and you shouldn't feel too badly about it. He'd got himself into a hell of a mess, and something like this was liable to happen at any time. Don't let it be on your conscience.'

'You may keep me on your conscience for as long as you like,' Toby said. 'I doubt if either of you has yet grasped how cleft my stick would have been. She had me coming and going; first, to plant the fraudulent evidence, and then to blackmail me about it. It is the last time I shall accept a recommendation from you, Tessa.'

'I don't blame you, and I suppose Julian would agree. He was the biter bit, though.'

'You think he did recognise her, in spite of all that business with the handkerchief?'

'Certain of it. He never forgot a face, or a detail, that was detrimental in some way; and he was in such wild spirits, immediately afterwards. I couldn't account for it, at the time, but it could well have been that, recognising her and seeing how terrified she was, he thought he was on the track of something nastier than even he had ever managed to rake up before. The thrill was short-lived, though, poor old Julian. What's more, I believe now that he was actually trying to warn me about her, when he rang up, in his last throes.'

'But, Tessa dear, you always insisted that he never mentioned any name except Barnes.'

'Yes, but I may have underrated him. Just at the end, it sounded as though he was calling for help, but, as I've told you, his voice was terribly blurred, and it might have been "Phelps" that he was trying to say. That really is the only way to account for his ringing me up at all, at such a moment. Perhaps it means that he was genuinely quite fond of me, after all.'

'Let's hope you're right,' Robin said. 'It would be comforting to believe that he performed at least one altruistic deed in his life. Well, here's to crime!' he added, raising his glass. 'Coupled, as I pray God for the last time, with our beloved Tessa!'

'He'd be in a right old mess without me, though,' I said to Toby. 'Shall I tell you something? He actually began to suspect Betty, just at the time when I knew for certain that she couldn't have done it. It was the day we came back from Warwickshire. He got some crazy idea in his head that she'd driven up to London at crack of dawn and murdered Sebastian, having pinched the front door key out of my bag. After that, she was supposed to have driven all the way back to the hotel again, and sailed in, pretending she'd been for a country walk. I ask you!'

'It's not so silly,' Robin said stiffly. 'She could have done just that. We went over the route, and it was perfectly feasible.'

'Oh, feasible! What's the good of that? Psychologically, it was all wrong. For one thing, she absolutely rejected my theory about Jasmine being a murderess. If she'd been guilty, herself, she'd have snatched at the chance of someone else taking the rap. All right, what have I said now, to give you both hysterics? Surely, you know what taking the rap means?'

'It's not that which set us off,' Robin explained, after a few more cackles of mirth. 'But you've hit on the very circumstance which made the police think seriously about her, all over again.'

'For God's sake, why?'

'It's so simple, darling. You see, for an innocent person, it would have been so much more natural at least to have given some consideration to your Jasmine theory. Why not? It was all right, as far as it went. On the other hand, if Betty were guilty, Jasmine would have been the last scapegoat she'd have wanted.'

'Why? She wasn't all that fond of her.'

'No, but she'd have been well aware that we should connect the second murder with the first. At that stage, only the murderer knew that the second one had already been committed; and Jasmine was out of the running for that, with half a dozen witnesses to prove it. Understand now?'

'Yes. Yes, I do. Stupid of me not to have seen it. Oh well, we can't all be wise, after the event, any more than before; and none of that is really important. What counts is my once telling you that I could never be friends with a murderer; not real friends like I am with Betty. I went right off Sandy, at the end. It's these inner voices of ours which do so much to bring criminals to justice.'